# Patriarch(
# Y'sra'el's right-]
# Methods a.

### By Rabbi Simon Altaf

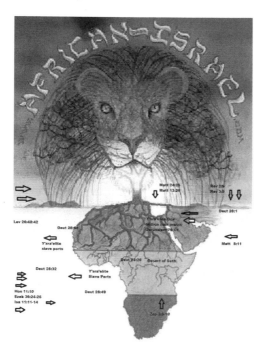

Copyright©2012 13, Jan 2012 African-Y'sra'el International Qahalim

Revised 9, Dec 2013

Excerpts can be used from this book without modification for study or reprinting purposes with the set condition that as long as reference is given back to the author and this book.

Rebbe Simon Altaf, BM African-Y'sra'el, London WC1N 3XX, England (UK)

For contacting us the USA Rebbe Lamont Clophus, African-Y'sra'el, 8111 Mainland, Suite 104-152, San Antonio, Texas, 78240, USA

For contacting us in UK Rebbe Simon Altaf for African-Y'sra'el International Union of Qahalim or please contact us via e-mail through africanysrael@yahoo.com or phone in the UK +44 (0) 1296 48 27 95 or phone Rebbe Lamont in the USA: Tel 1-210-827-3907.

**Africa**

Our African contact for all registered Synagogues affiliated to African-Y'sra'el International please contact us.

**Other**

Failure to get in contact with any of the above people please contact Rabbi Simon Altaf directly in the UK +44 (0) 1296 48 27 95, leave your message and he will contact you but please do leave a clear contactable telephone number with the international telephone code. Or e-mail africanysrael@yahoo.com. Thank you.

Visit our website at: www.african-israel.com

All quotes are from the Hidden-Truths Hebraic Scrolls unless otherwise stated.

# Table of Contents

Introduction .................................................................... 4

## CHAPTER 1 .................................................. 7
The Proverbs 31 woman ............................................... 7

## CHAPTER 2 .................................................. 21
Fornication or Whoring what should it be? ............... 21

## CHAPTER 3 .................................................. 79
Ancient pattern of North and South placement ........ 79

## CHAPTER 4 .................................................. 93
Polygany or Monogamy what was Y'sra'el's true lifestyle? ....... 93

## CHAPTER 5 .................................................. 118
Questions and Objections ........................................... 118

## CHAPTER 6 .................................................. 153
World's government systems versus YHWH's Torah government ............................................................. 153

## CHAPTER 7 .................................................. 167
Marriage is not an Enterprise .................................... 167
   Additional questions that need answers ................ 197

## Introduction

Other authors have written about this subject but this subject still remains in somewhat mysterious waters and many Torah right-ruling men and women are confused about its application. The reason why the confusion still remains is because the various authors generally talking about the polygyny but not enough detailed explanation has been given for the way the system was actually practiced. Also the fact that many western authors who have little knowledge of Ysra'el's Eastern history and practices have tried to invent new ways to practice it, which at times are at odds with the ancient practices and sometimes the modern methods simply fail to work. This author sets the record straight what was and still is biblical polygyny and how it was practiced. Many other questions arise such as what is the first wife's role, what and how is the husband to behave in all this with his various wives. The answers though lie in the Torah but the application is not very visible without a knowledgeable explanation of the past, which is now going to be illuminated here to some extent to help you from a son of Y'sra'el from the east.

Some of the things that sometimes are taught by Western authors as a caution is to ask your spouse before you go to marry your second wife; this is not a requirement or a commandment. A husband who is right-ruling tells his wife and does not need to ask for permission this is where many are going wrong. The idea that somehow you ask belittles the man he is the authority of the home and not the woman so we need to pay attention that right-ruling women listen and pay heed to their husband's and not become the one's in the authority. This is what I mean by western flawed authorship and practice of plural marriage which is at odds with our practices of true Y'sra'elites.

In Y'sra'elite history and culture there was no such thing as asking permission from your spouses. A wife who ties herself to you is to tie to you in complete faith and love and you as a right-ruler are meant to love her and to support all her needs throughout her life to the very end of her life. Marriage is a Contract Agreement between two parties or two families and the contractual terms stated is the death of one or other party this is how ancient contracts/covenants were cut. However today just because your spouse did not like something you said to her much worse the western mind has adopted western serial monogamy in which you marry one wife and then divorce her to acquire another or perhaps she does not want you to obtain another is simply the spirit of Lilith in women of that evil woman spoken of in Genesis 1:27 which was regenerated by the light of Satan as co-equal with Adam but fell from favor.

The practice of asking women is unheard of in the pages of scripture. It's <u>also</u> unlawful according to the law of God as I will demonstrate here. What is the role of the second wife and how is she supposed to behave, whose children will have the family inheritance. What about a place to stay and how do you accommodate this? What about placing the wives in one city or two cities even two countries and what direction and how this affects marriages spiritually. What about the woman who is adamant that she wants to be monogamous only and many other questions are now to be addressed.

Do you think Rabbi Tarfon perhaps asked his one northern wife for the 300 wives so they do not starve to death?

Rabbi Tarfon married 300 women when there was a famine in the land of Y'sra'el, these were not his only wives. He was a kohen and received the priestly tithe so could afford to feed all his wives and believe me they were so grateful that a Lewite took them as wives. They were even more grateful that the Torah permitted this unlike today's many wayward gentile women. (See the Talmud Yevamot 4:12.)

    The reason for this book is to explain the application of Torah polygyny and how it was worked in the ancient times, how it would once again work if both men and women are submitted to YHWH. The reality is this that where there is no submission there is no law but only a shadow of it and this is the state of many places today in the world where both men and women are running wild with all being kings and queens of their own fickle imaginations but when the Messiah Yahushua returns the shadows will be gone but the reality will be in place. Disobedience can cost one his earthly life and at worst even his redemption but obedience can extend your life by many years, the question is do you want to lose your life over wrong choices.

All references will be taken from the Hidden-Truth Hebraic Scrolls unless otherwise stated.

> **Yeshayahu (Isa) 4:1** And in that day seven women shall take hold of one man, saying, we will eat our own lechem (bread), and wear our own apparel: only let us be called by your name, to take away our reproach.[1]

This by the way is the ideal number of wives a man can and should have provided he can afford them all. This does not mean ancient Y'sra'elites did not marry more women they did but it was according to their means.

---

[1] In the End of Days because of wars there will be a huge surplus of women and seven women will be married to one man. This is Biblical accepted polygamy and not an allegory as some deliberately tried to hide the Y'sra'elite lifestyle and corrupt it with their western Greek serial monogamy.

# Chapter 1
## *The Proverbs 31 woman*

**Mishle (Pro) 31:10** Who can find a virtuous woman? For her price is far above rubies.

The famous Proverbs 31 chapter and the woman described within it is of a polygynous household which is the real biblical patriarchy. Monogamy is of Satan who causes men and women to divorce to do serial marriage because he has one wife the whore of Babylon (Rev 17:1), while Y'sra'elites had more than one wife the character of the lion. So which will you be a lion or a wolf?

This is why many women are already deceived in the western world with the spirit of Lilith who think they are right and others are wrong. This problem is not only in the West but it also exists in the east in many countries that have adopted western colonial practices.

This should knock you back a little because most people had thought the Proverbs 31 woman was a monogamous household and all women wanted to be the Proverbs 31 woman however truth be told this is not the case as it's the complete opposite to what many think out there. Now how many women want to obey YHWH and go the proverbs 31 route? First all women put their hands up but when I tell them this woman is polygynous then suddenly I don't see any hands.

The woman in Proverbs 31 was one of the principle wife's and she had the other secondary wives in the household who she was not jealous of since she did not have the spirit of jealousy and she served her husband with right-ruling ways. However many women today cannot control their jealousy and anger which reveals they have a lot of petitions to do to ask for shalom in their lives in order to serve their earthly master, the husband, followed by their spiritual Master the Messiah Yahushua. Any woman who cannot serve her earthly husband can certainly not serve Melek Yahushua, she is living in la-la land thinking she can because submission starts with your earthly husband. If you cannot submit to your earthly husband there is no chance you can serve Melek Yahushua so stop lying to yourself and others when you say you are serving Yahushua when it was the God of Y'sra'el who ordained patriarchal marriages and revealed it in Himself.

> **Mishle (Pro) 31:11** The heart of her husband does safely trust in her, so that he shall have no need of spoil.

The good principle wife does not go or plan to slander her husband when he has or is about to take on another wife that he can afford and will be given money to afford by YHWH but the husband trusts in his wife and other wives to be the complete trustees over his household and children. There are certain books written putting polygyny down such as "Wife number 19" by a Mormon woman who was wed in a plural marriage in the Church of the Latter Day Saints which abused women in the wrong ways hence why women were oppressed yet we are not going to do some kind of witch-hunt against Mormonism or polygyny while many wrong practices exist in Mormonism but their greater sin was not polygamy but removing themselves from the real Father YHWH in heaven to worship a false father and a false Jesus of the west, the Caucasian variety while the real Yahushua is Black and African looking, see my book "Yahushua – The Black Messiah.

> **Mishle (Pro) 31:12** She will do him good and not evil all the days of her life.

Unfortunately all man-made religions took our Y'sra'elite Torah government truths and modified it to create their religions, the Mormons were not wrong about polygyny because YHWH is polygamous but the method of polygyny by the Mormon's was somewhat inaccurate and its application was not according to the Torah.

Having more wives is a great benevolence of YHWH upon the men of Y'sra'el. The wives are meant to support and build the kingdom of YHWH.

**Ezekiel 23:1, 2, 4** The word of YHWH came again to me, saying, **2** Son of man, there were two women, the daughters of one mother: **4** And the names of them were Aholah the elder, and Aholibah her sister: and they were my *wives*, and they bore sons and daughters. Thus were their names; Shomeron (Samaria) is Aholah, and Yerushalim Aholibah.

The two wives of YHWH, since YHWH is the first recorded Patriarch and revealer of Patriarchal marriage and the one who appointed this. The pattern of the **North** and **South** revealed in YHWH. Now there goes our so called Modern culture out of the window. In drash (allegory) YHWH declared himself husband to His two wives (Y'sra'el) He was married to them under Mount Sinai. These are the two houses of Y'sra'el, one placed in the North and the other in the South. This is the perfect pattern. Now a man should not place both wives in the same house unless it's for a short duration only if big enough but the pattern revealed is to place them in the city or cities North and South in relation to the man since the North represents the place of heavens where Abbah YHWH dwells. A man can put a wife in two sections of the same house such as upstairs flat and downstairs flat so that can also be the North and the South.

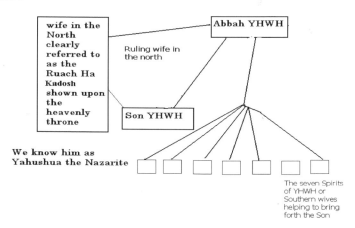

So if YHWH is a Patriarch and reveals what should be the Proverbs 31 woman then you as a woman need to ask are you that woman and if not then why not. The man needs to ask is he a Torah right-ruling man or just a man of the street who doesn't care what YHWH the

God of Y'sra'el declares as His truth but who perhaps carries on doing his own thing to his detriment.

The twelve tribes of Y'sra'el came from Yaqub (Jacob) and his four wives. Are you as a serial monogamist ashamed of this? I am not. Great men of Y'sra'el had many wives who were a great help to their husbands. More than one pair of hands is always better in the home both with the children and without children. Many wives add to the man in many ways while also they help to suppress one wife trying to rule the husband. In other words more than one wife is a good measure to suppress women as rulers to tone them down.

Now look at the culture where you live and see how much disobedience you all live in.

If the spouses don't like what their husband said they run to the divorce court but this never happened with Y'sra'elite women. So if you have railed against your husband and put him down to elevate yourself then its time to repent and time to mend your ways or you will face the end of your life with judgment and banishment. In true Hebrew repentance you do not run to the pagan churches but you first go to the man or woman you wronged and then come before Abbah YHWH and ask for forgiveness in the name of the Master Yahushua. It is only then that you can be forgiven.

## The role of the first wife

Many women ask what the role of the first wife is. If one looks carefully at the Proverbs 31 woman the example is given of how the first wife behaves towards the others maidservants (secondary wives).

> **Mishle (Pro) 31:15** She rises also while it is yet night, and gives food to her household, and a portion to her maidens.

The role of the first is quite clear. No jealousy is found in her towards the other maids (wives) who are acquired by her husband. She is a faithful woman and needs to remain faithful and loving to the husband. She is to make sure that an arrangement is made with her husband before he acquires any secondary wives that there is enough provision in the household to accommodate them all. Also a husband has to decide how his many wives will operate. This does not mean that all this man's wives lived in one house it does mean he had wives living in a number of households as he was an important political figure.

If the husband struggles to provide for the first wife then how can he ever acquire the other wives and support them? Does that mean he has to defer the second/third marriages until the time he has sufficient income to cater for the wives?

No, he does not, now let me tell you a secret. Each woman is allotted an increase when she is born so the man that marries her will get that increase. In other words as soon as you step into the additional marriage you will acquire the increase therefore you will be able to easily acquire an additional wife. The problem is that you think too much with your head and lack trust in YHWH. Trust YHWH and He will make the provision. More on this later.

A man can decide what is his threshold of how many wives he should ultimately acquire, the principle wife's duty is to help her husband fulfill the role of kingdom building through right-ruling children. The number seven is mentioned as the ideal number of wives in scripture. However not all men can afford seven wives therefore one has to decide on the ideal number according to their make up and as I said earlier even if you do not have the income it shall be provided from above provided you are a right-ruling man.

So the choices you make of how many depends on what level of wives you can maintain both physically and spiritually.

Since the first wife is the principle wife she will have to make arrangement in discussion with her husband what time he spends with his secondary wives and the ultimate goal in acquiring further wives is usually to increase the right-ruling seed in Y'sra'el but there can be other important goals such as increasing the Kingdom of Y'sra'el or if the man is involved in some business in which his wives will aid him. This is seen in that the husband does not necessarily need to look at the additional wives to increase more children but he may be doing a direct effort to reach the nations with the Torah truth and the Black Messiah of Y'sra'el. His additional wives therefore could be assisting him in this work while the first has to be in charge of household affairs such as bills, to make sure she has a hold of the finances and knows what monies are needed to purchase groceries, pay bills in which the husband will set an allowance to give her each month. In addition, the husband will then allocate any further expenses for additional wives in their respective homes.

The first wife's role is to love her husband and respect his decision and to stand with him at all times and at all cost no matter what given the man is Torah obedient and not a careless wayward Hebrew. If for whatever reason the husband has made a wrong decision she is to stand by him and give guidance to him if she sees any pitfalls in any situation she is there as a monitor to assist. She is his helpmeet and the strength of that man.

**Mishle (Pro) 31:17** She **girds her loins with strength**, and **strengthens her arms**.

The expression "to strengthens her arms" here is not for her personal arms but for the other wives that are present in her husband's life to help them in order to help her husband to build the home. To be a guide and a listening ear for them as they may be immature in the ways of YHWH so the principle wife is to be the strong tower that the husband can turn to for helping the other wives in his homes so that they feel comfortable and are taken care of. Therefore by definition she is her husband's strength as I said earlier. This role belongs to the principle wife but if the principle wife is herself weak in the faith then it makes it harder for her to adopt with the other forthcoming wives. In which case she will need guidance from her rabbi/teacher to assist her in the matters of faith and how to deal with the household in right-ruling or the husband will have to teach her.

> **Mishle (Pro) 31:16** She considers a field, and buys it: with the fruit of her hands she plants a vineyard.

This is an indication that the first wife in ancient times was not just a household item but was an entrepreneur so she could get involved in some business practices. In the modern world this would be similar to her being involved in helping her husband in increasing the household income to supplement the income or being involved in an enterprise or business of some kind with the husband's guidance.

## What about the women who do not marry and want to do it on their own?

This is not commanded and all such women who are stuck in this pattern in the absence of the Temple are not serving God in the right way and are Torah violators, this is not acceptable as YHWH said it is not good for the man (Gen 2:18) to be alone and the same applies to the woman.

All women are to tie themselves to a right-ruling man and to seek to carry all the needs of the husband and God in the home. Those women who have the idea that they can tie themselves to a monogamous only man are simply living in their own fantasy world. All Torah men are capable of having and maintaining more than one wife and would just need direction on how to build this kind of household. Even the income takes care of itself if the women are submitted to God and to their husband the income is allotted from the heavens. The argument that a man is lustful is a foolish argument put by weak and unwise women, many men are capable and designed to handle more than one wife and having intimate relations with their wives is perfectly fine and not lustful in any way as it's a gift from God.

The word "lust" is the wrong word people have invented while the word always used in scripture is "need" and not lust. The word in the Hebrew is nefesh as used in Exodus 15:9, which is simply a word for the soul. The Greek word used to translate for 'lust' is the

Strong's G1937 epee-thoo-meho, which is used in Matthew 5:28 is more appropriate to be translated as 'desire'. So if you 'desire' another man's wife then it is considered adultery. While you may rightfully "desire" to have three wives and it is perfectly fine. What we have discovered in the absence of real Y'sra'elites taking part in the translation work of our scrolls the gentiles did very bad translations of our scrolls instead and have deceived our people. In the present translations a good word can also be made to look bad as the example of the word "lust" which should really be a "need" or "desire" depending on the context. In the correct context the word for 'lust' which is 'desire' is simply saying its wrong to 'desire' another man's wife, while the same word 'desire' can apply to polygyny where its not wrong to 'desire' two or more wives.

No Hebrew man is designed for one woman this is a fallacy. The following issues can arise with single women who choose to do it on their own and consider themselves an Island.

They may end up forming relations with single men who without marriage leave them with an empty promise to marry. They may leave them pregnant as is happening in many western cultures and in Africa common in Kenya. The women in the west become extremely bitter and start to hate all men. The woman after having the child will be hiding her past relationship from this child so that they cannot find his/her genetic father due to the bitterness of the woman.

As the child grows up the woman cannot be an example to the child especially if he is a male child. The son needs his father but the mother has likely been teaching the child to hate his father because he left this woman without marriage. She may also teach him more feminine traits than masculine so he has the wrong psychology. She would make him weaker rather than stronger.

This type of mother then tries to dictate the life of her son who grows up weak and with no real direction because the mother could not fulfill the job of the absent father. With a girl the girl has no real example and the direction of a father either. The mother can teach the girl the things of women but because of the hatred she teaches of the father the girl grows up hating men and ends up being dysfunctional.

The boy may grow up in two directions. One he ends up in the drug culture because he wants to belong, he has no role model so he tries to fit in with some local gangs. Furthermore, he is confused about his identity so he may hate women for what his mother did to him therefore he becomes rebellious. He may try to prove his manliness on other men through violence like he is getting back at his father who was absent all these years, while he has no respect left for women as a result of his mother's harsh upbringing.

His mother cannot stop him as he gets his way to get revenge from the world. The cycle simply perpetuates as he may also do the same as his father by finding a woman, impregnating her and leaving her to do the same to his children and we have the classical vicious cycle of another absentee father. This is actually a generational curse that needs to be broken.

The only way to get out of this cycle and the generational Torah curses is first for the woman to turn back to the Torah to repent of her sins followed by the child doing the same when he is older or at least twenty which is the only way to break this curse. The woman would do well to attach to a right-ruling man as a husband to allow some normalcy in her life and to have some stable relationship with her son. The woman or the man needs to ask for forgiveness from God and ask God to break the curse while the man can then start to obey the Torah which will bring the increases in his or her life very quickly.

The bottom line a woman cannot do it on her own she must tie into a marriage or concubine relationship to a man else her life will simply be miserable especially as she grows old with bitterness in her heart.

## What is a concubine?

A piligesh is simply a lesser form of marriage with no written ketubah (contract), since the Hebrew has no word for wife the word Ishah in Hebrew applies both to women generally and to a wife as well. A concubine is someone who ties herself to a man for a duration of time agreed between her and the man she is with and she can leave the man without an inheritance if she desires. She has no right to the inheritance neither do her children unless the man or husband gives her something by his own freewill. While a woman who marries legally with a ketubah has rights in the marriage. In the ancient Torah culture concubines usually stayed for life.

Those who even remotely suggest that the concubine is a whore just for sex in anyway are foolish to mock YHWH's laws promoting their so called monogamous agendas of the Greek and Roman Satanic kind. These kind of foolish statements usually come from women the least to know Torah laws are quite mistaken as in ancient times the concubines never left their husband, they were given houses to live and even land but the provision was there if they were not happy for any reason they could leave. In fact its fair to say modern marriages in the Church or any other system are concubine contracts therefore applying the definition of a whore that some ignorantly suggest this makes every church wife a whore also or one married in the state is the same. This is something to think about these kind of foolish statements. YHWH does not recognize the church or state contract so what does that make you? At least in a concubine Torah contract YHWH is in it.

All worldly contracts are concubine contracts. Let me explain, the Church has been wrong on this that a man and woman living together is sin. Any man and any single woman can live together but their arrangement is simply seen as a husband and a concubine (lesser wife without a contract). Any worldly contracts that men form such as marrying a woman through a marriage license via any man-made ceremonies are not seen or counted by YHWH. Here is how it works. Here are some examples to think about.

If two Hindus married does the God of Y'sra'el recognize that marriage? Answer, No.

If two Muslims married using the Islamic system does the God of Y'sra'el recognize that marriage. The answer again is No.

If two Ysra'elites married does the God of Y'sra'el recognize the marriage? The answer is Yes, this is because when they get married legally according to the Torah they had a rabbi/elder present, they had a ketubah, a legal document prepared and most of all the God of Y'sra'el and his name were invoked in the marriage. The same is true for the Torah concubine contract which is verbally invoked.

Jesus the western appellation of the Messiah is not the name of God but YHWH is. The Messiah's real name is Yahushua. Even if you get married in a Church system that piece of paper is still not recognized in the heavens since they never invoked God's real name and neither do they uphold the Torah. So what you are doing is simply a worldly contract between two people.

God only becomes the third person to stand in the marriage as a witness when it is His people involved who are under his Contract hence why God recognizes only this relationship where the man formulates the contract invoking his name. While in the example given above of the Muslim, the Hindu, the Christian or secular marriage YHWH is not invoked nor recognized therefore how can he be party to a marriage in which idolaters are getting married. OK, it may be that the men and women in such marriages don't know God through no fault of their own but still that marriage is not recognized by the God of Y'sra'el. Hence all such human contracts whether verbal or written are nothing more than concubinage in which only two parties are involved. So in such cases if a woman left the man or the man left the woman there is no repercussion. The heavens do not care but personal sins will still be counted within such people.

Let's analyze this further.

If a Catholic man and a Catholic woman married according to the Catholic Church formula does the God of Y'sra'el recognize that marriage? It's clear the answer is No, since God did not form the Catholic Church nor does he recognizes any such authority the Pope carries or claims. Therefore any such marriages even in which people bind and receive a piece of paper from the Catholic Church for the marriage is nothing more than a concubine marriage.

If you go to a court and get married in a court system what is called a registrar marriage the same applies, it's simply a contract between a man and woman hence a concubine arrangement. God has no part in it. The only way the God of Y'sra'el has any part in a marriage is if you invoke him, his sacred name and his sacred laws in the marriage and the marriage is according to the laws (Torah) of Musa in which case a ketubah is drawn up in which a rabbi or an elder signs it and two witnesses are present who are present to sign the contract which also believe in YHWH. That is a marriage in the eyes of God in which He has entered the contract with the male and female under oath in God's set-apart name YHWH. In a concubine contract sworn verbally the man and the woman are recognized by the God of Y's'ra'el since they are under Contract with him bound in His Torah laws.

**Registrar marriage and the State laws**

Unless you want to get a marriage license for purposes of State law one should avoid getting bogged down with this and a marriage should simply be conducted under the laws of Torah. This way you can marry first the one wife followed by others and you avoid the laws of bigamy that the State enforces upon you. If you ever have to use the court system then just only register one of your wives this way the State cannot prosecute you for bigamy. For the rest of your wives you should take them under Torah law. By getting stuck into the State laws you are putting yourself under risk of these gentile laws that we are not to use to be in contract with as we were told do not form covenants with the gentiles but many of you have not learnt your lesson yet.

> **Deut 7:2** And when YHWH your Elohim shall hand them before you; You shall conquer them, and utterly destroy them; You shall make no Contract/Agreement with them, nor show loving-kindness to them:
>
> **Matt 10:5** These twelve Yahushua sent forth, and commanded them, saying, do not get into the way of the heathens, and into any cities[2] of the Samaritans do not enter:

**The way:** - Pagan practices from the Aramaic. You have YHWH's WAY or the Pagan 'way.' Most Christians today live in Pagan practices, which are incompatible with YHWH's WAY.

**Essentially we are forbidden to go into Contracts/Agreements with the gentiles as they bind us in ways that forbids us from practicing the Torah laws.**

While we see many such Christians who do not obey the Torah are quite happy to make covenants with the gentiles and to marry according to the gentiles. Hence why it is forbidden for us Y'sra'elites to do such practices and we must be mindful of what we have been told and commanded earlier in the Torah and also by Melek Yahushua.

Simply put anytime you bind yourself to state or country law you are stuck and then you cannot unbind that very easily without going through costly exercises. What if you married according to your state law that forbids two wives and now you want to have two wives? In this instance only two possibilities exist, one is to undo the state marriage through a state divorce which has really no consequence on your matrimony in the

---

[2] The Aramaic has plural cities instead of city. The Samaritans had many cities. Yahushua wanted to start the re-gathering process himself so that is why we see him talking to the Samaritan prophetess in Yahuchannan (John) 4:7. He knew that his disciples may be hostile to the Samaritans because of the prevalent hatred.

sight of YHWH provided you are married by the laws of Torah with a ketubah (A Torah marriage contract). For a concubine this does not apply. In the case of the Torah as long as you do not bind yourself to the State laws you can marry any number of wives you are able to provide for. YHWH did not put a limit but only men did though he did show an ideal number to be seven.

Note also your State contract is not binding in the heavens it has no validity whatsoever so whether you have it or not it's of no consequence above while its usefulness is only of value here on the earth with your governments to authenticate and show that you are bound to your state. Y'sra'elites are not going to be stopped from practicing their YHWH given lifestyle by any State law but practice it according to the Torah with understanding so you do not mess women around if you do not obey the Torah. In Jamaica even though the British put their laws in place but many people continued to practice polygyny by calling the second wife the baby's mother with no contract. In affect they proved the British are not going to stop the Y'sra'elites from practicing marriage with more than one woman. The Jamaicans are not Jamaicans but Y'sra'elites, many I Jamaica are from the tribe of Yissachar.

# Chapter 2
## *Fornication or Whoring what should it be?*

A lot of people are confused about this and do not understand the difference between fornication or whoring. The word <u>fornication</u> is a newly invented word and is misapplied to marital situations.

> **Acts 15:29** That you abstain from meats offered to idols, and from blood, and from things strangled, and from <u>whoring</u>: from which if you keep yourselves, you shall do well[3]. Fare well.

This word used in Acts 15:29 in your bibles is likely "fornication" but it should not be fornication but either idolatry or whoring G4202 for the Greek word Pornia.

The correct Hebrew term for whoring is Strong's H2181 Zanaw which would be the equivalent term for the Greek retranslation of the Hebrew in Acts 15:29. The same word that is used for 'whoring' Strong's G4202 is the same word used in Matthew 5:32 to describe 'whoring.' Therefore to use the term "fornication" instead of whoring is inaccurate and wrong see the Hidden-Truths Hebraic Scrolls for the correct terms.

> **Matt 5:32** But I say to you, that whosoever shall put away his wife, unless for the cause of <u>whoring</u>, causes her to commit adultery and whosoever shall marry her that is undivorced commits adultery.

The King James Version incorrectly uses the term 'fornication', in both instances which does not satisfy the Torah requirement of divorce.

---

[3] This was minimum basics to join the community but this did not mean that they were not to keep the Sabbath or the feasts as all things were done in order once they learned how to do them which would be fairly quickly as they read Torah and understood the principles each week on the Sabbath on Friday night in the Synagogues.

How do you then apply the term 'fornication' in the context of Acts 15:29? You cannot because are you saying you can fornicate with an animal or how do you apply the term 'whoring'? The easiest is to understand that to offer an animal to a false god would be 'whoring' and not fornicating. This unfortunate error exists in Christendom in the majority of their text.

The dictionary describes the word fornication as follows:

Voluntary sexual intercourse between two unmarried persons or two persons not married to each other.

- Idolatry

This is how the term fornication is meaningless and has no place as a term in the sacred scrolls. It was an invented term and has caused many people to be confused. According to the Torah if two people let's say a married man and a single unmarried woman on mutual consent had sexual intercourse together she would become his concubine and therefore the modern dictionary term would apply the meaning of "fornication" which is both false and inaccurate.

See the case in point of Hagar while Abraham did not break any law of YHWH as it was and it still is perfectly legal according to Torah to have a concubine and have consensual sex with her as long as she is not married or another man's concubine. Today, in Churches countless Pastors have been thrown out wrongly for fornication when they have done nothing wrong by having consensual sex with a single unmarried woman when they became enamored, which would be classed as a concubine relation in the old days and according to the law of God even today.

One may ask but if you have a wife and a concubine then can you just have sexual contact with your concubine and then discard her or perhaps move on to another? The answer is no in that when you tie a verbal contract with a concubine in which you did not do a big marriage ceremony she is still your wife and you do not discard her once you have had enough of her. In ancient times concubines were bound to you forever there were very few cases where a concubine would leave her husband since she was still considered and applied the title of wife. Note in the Hebrew there is no title for wife but only woman such as Ishah. It is the same term that we translate as wife due to context of the verse but the term literally means 'woman.'

This is given the modern meaning of wife but this is not its ancient meaning so a woman was simply somebody we today call a wife who tied herself to a man with a contract cut by blood. The same was true with a concubine who tied herself to the man forever with a verbal contract Hagar is an interesting case in point. Even though Hagar the Egyptian black princess was removed from Abraham's home in the North what people forget is that she went to the south in Beersheba and lived there Gen 21:14 and Abraham continued to have relations with her.

In gen 21:20 we are told that God was with Y'shma'el while many folks in the churches make out as if Abraham had no dealings with them any more this is simply not true. Hagar continued to be Abrahams' wife and he visited her often as his other wife Keturah was also in Beersheba with her six sons and daughters. In fact the correct translation of the Hebrew in Gen 25:1 tells us Abraham spent more time in Beersheba after the death of Sarah in which case he was close to all three of his wives Keturah, Hagar and Mashek.

> **Gen 25:1** And Henceforth Abraham continued with his wife, and her name was Keturah.

The error of not to be married or to have concubines is one that came from the so called Christian Church which practiced plural marriage and the taking of concubines until the 4$^{th}$ century CE.

Then the laws and decrees came from ascetics and stoics which many Christians are following to this day.

> **[7]At the council of Toledo, in A.D. 400, it was ordered, by canon seventeenth, that every Christian that had both a wife and a**

> concubine should be excommunicated; but he should not be excommunicated who had only a concubine without a wife. At the fourth council of Carthage, A.D. 401, it was ordered, by canon seventieth, that all bishops, priests, and deacons, who had wives, must repudiate them, and live in celibacy, under penalty of deposition from office. Pope Innocent I., about A.D. 412, in his official letter to the two bishops of Abruzzo, orders them to depose those priests who had been guilty of the crime of having children since their ordination. Thus the seeds of Gnostic error that had been sown in the church during the former periods of its history, now sprang up anew, and bore a plentiful harvest.

[7] The History and Philosophy of Marriage, Or, Polygamy and Monogamy Compared 1869 page 132 by James Campbell

From this one can see why the term concubine and fornication brings both confusion and error.

Question, if a man has sexual relations with an unmarried and unattached woman he is not married to her then is he fornicating or in reality whoring?

Answer) Christians are taught to say the man is fornicating which is incorrect the man is not whoring. He could be married or single and has a perfect Torah right to have consensual relations with the woman with a verbal contract.

Since the woman is in relation with the man in question with her consent this relationship falls in the category of a concubine relationship and the term fornication is not even appropriate because if you remember the example above the right term for fornication would be "whoring" and you cannot "whore" with an unmarried woman who has relations with a man with consent. A woman can only "whore" when she sleeps at the same time with several different men while tied in a relationship with a man. A man can only "whore," while he is bowing down to false gods. He cannot whore having sexual relations with several women who are his concubines or even single women in sexual relations with him in consent. If you try to apply the confused and erroneous term 'fornication' from the modern dictionary's usage then it would unfairly apply to Melek Dawud with his eighteen wives and also to Abraham making them both transgressors but they were not. So where does it stop? This is why one must not use the false Christian label which is much misunderstood even amongst Christians who lack Torah understanding.

A man cannot whore with two single women or three single women since he can be a husband to all three either in a Torah marriage or they can be his concubines by Torah law. Hence why one can see that the term 'fornication' cannot be applied at all. The Christian definition of "adultery" of a married man having intimate relations with a single woman is plainly wrong also. They will tell you that a man who has a wife and then has another relation with a single woman is adulterous. This is not the definition of adultery according to the Torah. A man with a wife and a concubine can have intimate relations with her and is perfectly legal according to the Torah and allowed. Adultery would only occur if the man had relations with someone else's wife.

> **Lev 18:20** Moreover You shall not lie carnally with your neighbour's wife, to defile yourself with her.

This is the 7$^{th}$ Commandment;

> **Exodus 20:14** You shall not commit adultery.

To adulterate means to mix seed. Any woman/wife can only have one husband at a time to allow them to have sexual intimacy in order to produce heirs. Two men as in two husbands such as in polyandry are forbidden from mixing their seed with the same woman that is tied in a relationship to her husband. Therefore it is quiet clear a single woman having intimate relations with a married man is not mixing seed as the man is the only one who carried the seed to produce the children. A married man is allowed to have more than one wife and is allowed to sleep with a single woman while being married with consent of that woman. The consent would make the relationship a concubine relationship which is allowed in the Torah. When Abraham took on Princess Hagar as his concubine no ceremonies are recorded in the Torah it just says Sarah gave Hagar to Abraham in which case it's clear the contract was verbal only and Hagar stayed with Abraham for life though a small party would have been given in the home by Abraham's servants to celebrate the relationship of Abraham and Hagar.

Princess Hagar was a better wife than most western women are today since she never departed from her husband willfully even when he told her to go though reluctantly she went but she never seek to divorce him. Now here is the prime example of a faithful eastern woman that would shame all the western women running after divorces breaking up homes.

The same definition was given by Melek Yahushua in Matthew 5:32.

> **Matt 5:32** But I say to you, that whosoever shall put away his wife, unless for the cause of whoring, causes her to commit adultery and whosoever shall marry her that is undivorced commits adultery.

So how does it cause a woman to commit adultery and the man that married a divorced woman to be in adultery? The KJV has an incorrect translation where the word should be undivorced and not divorced. A woman who is not divorced properly meaning for the cause of "whoring" is still married to the original husband so a piece of paper from the local court system does not free her. Therefore the next man that comes along to marry her is really taking a married woman and having relations with her which is the cause of the adulterating of the seed and puts both the man and woman in adultery. A woman must acquire a Get or she is not properly divorced remembering what I said earlier about what is valued in heaven and what is not. The national divorce court papers of all nations are worthless just as their marriage licenses. YHWH does not recognize them. However he recognizes a GET (A proper Torah document issued by a rabbi for a divorce in accordance with the law of God).

If the woman was divorced for "whoring" which means she was involved with another single or married man while being married then that is the only requirement for her husband to divorce her. This is not to say he cannot forgive her but it is to say he can divorce her for this reason alone. This is the actual proper reason for a divorce. There can be other reasons too in which a marital covenant/contract is violated such as injustice. A rabbi can then issue a Get (a divorce document) which means the woman is legal to remarry without any issues as she is no longer attached to her previous husband.

> **Lev 19:19** You shall keep my statutes. You shall not allow different animals to cross breed: You shall not sow your field with mixed seed: neither shall a garment mixed of linen and woolen come upon you.

As can be seen the principle carries and is applied here with no cross breading in which you are mixing two diverse seeds of two different animals that is forbidden. You are not allowed to sow two different seed in the same field and you are not allowed to mix two different clothes such as linen and cotton. Now if you imagine a woman to be a field then you can understand the concept that only one seed (One man) is to be planted in her in other words sexual relations can only exist with one man who she is attached with. She cannot go and allow herself to be intimately connected to two different men. This is polyandry and forbidden in the Torah.

The next question arises are men today allowed to have concubines?

The answer is self evidentiary in my explanation before. Since YHWH"s law is end to end and forever a concubine is as much allowed today as she was in the past. Note the method of the contract with the concubine is verbal only and it is between you and your concubine what you decide together as the Torah gives no formal or latter qualifications or requirements for the contract. Most people in the west who cohabit without a State marriage are actually living in a concubine type contract relationship because they have verbally agreed to live together and share the home, children and other things. Technically, the woman has no right to any of the man's property or wealth but because of local or national country laws women seem to get the upper hand and men the boot in these societies often losing the homes they have spent a lifetime building up.

If this was a Y'sra'elite man and woman then the terms would be agreed before hand a bit like a prenuptial agreement and then the couple would live together and work it out between themselves. A man can be married officially with a ketubah contract and have concubines depending on his finances. All marriages that are formed outside the Torah law without a Ketubah are simply seen as concubine relations in the eyes of YHWH. He does not endorse any of the gentile State marriage licenses since he forbids us from entering or making agreements with the gentiles. The principle must follow.

> **Deut 7:16** And You shall conquer all the people which YHWH your Elohim shall give you; your eye shall have no pity upon them: neither shall You serve their powers; for that will be a trap for you.

Any power, gods of the gentiles or gentile authority that can bind us and that includes their marriage laws, licenses etc have no real value for us apart from validating our marriage to the State. Powers in the above text can also be related to men who hold authority to enforce certain State laws that can trap us from breaking YHWH's commandments. So for instance if you had tied into a gentile contract for marriage then the law in that nation such as USA or Europe say that after having one wife you are forbidden to have another wife registered in the state is problematic for Torah men who wish to take another wife.

So by binding yourself to the State contract you have now entrapped yourself also in which in order to acquire another wife you have to either remove the State contract and divorce your wife by State law and keep her married to you by Torah law which is superior and then you are allowed to marry another. In which case it is simply that you undo your State marriage but before you do so make sure to have a Torah contract with your wife then the state cannot bind you to any of their laws and prosecute you. In this scenario you are allowed to have your extra wives but making sure to always only enact a Torah contract and never a state law so you do not become entrapped exactly what Deut 7:16 has said. The question may also arise what if I wanted to bring in my wife from another country in which case you need the state contract to do so. In that case the man or woman may do so in order to bring in their spouse but after the matter has been settled they may remove the state contract which allows them Torah freedom.

To most of the Western world marriage is simply a bond between a male and female of love (Eros) and mutual understanding and has nothing to do with what we term biblical commitment or the biblical model of marriage as a Contract/Covenant. The biblical model required a life long commitment and is a **CONTRACT** that can not be annulled in the lifetime of the two bonded together unless it was for very special circumstances that were allowed by the Rabbis but very few would like to understand TRUTH as stated in Scripture in the world of quick divorce AND remarriage.

Today in marriages if at anytime any incompatibilities or problems occur the first thing a couple look for is how to get out with a divorce and cut the tie so to speak. They do not look to reconcile or compromise with the husband or wife but instantly issue the threat that he/she is going to divorce you. Some couples may seek to reconcile but most do not give much thought to it and break the marriage without any due diligence or Scriptural wisdom. The church today compounds the problem by giving thumbs up to a situation that God hates (Mal 2:16). An average marriage in the Western world lasts for only about two years for normal couples and less than one year for celebrities. You can count yourself fortunate if your marriage lasted anything above two years. The divorce rate in the UK is the highest in Europe showing us how protestant England faired a lot worse than Catholic France or Italy.

The reason why the Catholics faired better was simply because they would not allow divorce under any circumstances forcing the couple to realign and live together. A separation in marriage was allowed but never a divorce unless as stated for special reasons and this is true with them believing Paul as stated in 1 Corinthians 7:11 however we do not follow Paul but YHWH and his guidelines. This was one of the primary reasons why Catholic England became protestant England during King Henry the VIII's reign, because of his marital issues and the reluctance of the Catholic Church to allow him a second marriage. The Catholic Church erred on its position at that time by not allowing King Henry VIII to add another wife without divorce as Biblically he could add more wives (Deut 21:15) without divorcing any of his previous wives. The Catholic Church adopted one position which was true but rejected the other due to the influence of Roman and Greek pagan cultures.

Tragically this enforced serial model of Roman/Greek monogamy ruined many women's lives during this period and is still ruining many lives today of children without fathers and wives without husbands.

Let us see how the Bible views the marriage CONTRACT?

Marriage is a <u>blood</u> CONTRACT and during the first night of a marriage when a couple consummate the marriage the woman's hymen is to break shedding blood to <u>establish</u> the Contract until one or the other party dies. You may ask how it can be everlasting if each man and woman has a finite life. The Contract terms were to last until the husband died because he is the head of authority not the woman hence the woman or wife was always recognized by her husband's name and so also the children acquired the father's name and not the mother's. This situation is the same today in many cultures.

To cut a covenant a Hebrew Brit it means one is saying that he will be there until he dies. This is why a kerituth in the Hebrew a breaking of that covenant would mean the end of cessation of life or in this case the putting away of the wife was really a serious matter. This is why in a divorce a couple is very distraught and it is like one has died.

We need to remember the CONTRACT terms are until DEATH and this is also what people recite RELIGIOUSLY in the west unless I am mistaken **UNTIL DEATH DO US PART** but to most of them who call themselves Christians or otherwise this does not mean DEATH but only a few months or a few years at best thus they cheat the husband or wife out of a CONTRACT agreement and commit adultery on either part. I understand the CONTRACT requires each party to do their bit in the marriage so it is not a FREE for all and for the men to subjugate the women in anyway or run off with another woman leaving her holding the children with no support system. The biblical laws have a support system for widows and for women generally. The man could also marry another woman while he provided a support system for the first wife.

> **Shemoth (Exo) 21:10** "If he takes another wife, he shall not diminish her food, her clothing, and her marriage rights.

Exodus is clear a man is allowed to add another wife/wives but he must provide for his wives'.

One may ask what if the woman today files for divorce perhaps in a situation where the man is insane or psychotic but here I believe the decision rests on the elders of the assembly to decide if it is safe to apply the divorce ruling immediately or wait since no man has the right to break the Contract. There are other factors for someone's psychosis whether it was induced as a result of illness or whether the husband defrauded the woman by not telling her in which case she can receive a Get (certificate of divorce) Deut 22:13-21.  This "certificate of divorce" needs to happen early in the marriage not ten years into the marriage unless special circumstances have caused the marriage to fail such as an unjust husband from who the wife feels threatened of serious injury or death!

The shedding of blood represents an everlasting Contract NEVER to be broken which means that the one consummating the marriage may be cut down and die if he/she was to break the Contract at any time in their life.  Do we see this in Scripture in any part of a Contract?  The answer is yes.

> **Gen 15:9-10** And He said to him, "Bring Me a three-year-old heifer, and a three year-old female goat, and a three-year-old ram, and a turtledove, and a young pigeon." (10) And he took all these to Him and cut them in the middle, and placed each half opposite the other, but he did not cut the birds.
>
> **Gen 15:17** And it came to be, when the sun went down and it was dark, that see, a **smoking oven and a burning torch passing between those pieces**.

In the near East kings made similar covenants known as suzerain treaties where a treaty was made and the names of the ones making the treaty were signified followed by increases if the vassal carried out the stipulations and curses if the Vassal did not!  The placing and cutting of animals in half signified death to the two parties and similar cutting as of the animals if anyone was to detract or not carry out the stipulation of the Contract.

> http://en.wikipedia.org/wiki/Suzerainty
>
> Suzerainty occurs where a region or people are a tributary to a more powerful entity which controls its foreign affairs while allowing the tributary vassal state some limited domestic autonomy.

Historically, the Emperor of China saw himself as the center of the entire civilized world, and diplomatic relations in East Asia were based on the theory that all rulers of the world derived their authority from the Emperor. The degree to which this authority existed in fact changed from dynasty to dynasty. However, even during periods when political power was distributed evenly across several political entities, Chinese political theory recognized only one emperor and asserted that his authority was paramount throughout the world. Diplomatic relations with the Chinese emperor were made on the theory of tributary states, although in practice tributary relations would often result in a form of trade under the theory that the emperor in his kindness would reward the tributary state with gifts of equal or greater value.

Abraham was put to sleep so God was fully responsible for bringing about the promises He made to Abraham and His seed.

In a marriage both parties the husband and wife are making a <u>blood</u> Contract. Men are allowed more than one wife so there should never be a question of divorce but polyandry is forbidden in the Bible so the woman has to accept that this is how God created her for man, not for men to abuse their authority. Scripture does not allow mixing of seed hence why polyandry is forbidden in the Scriptures.

The wife is to be submitted to her husband in love and not to usurp authority as many are doing today. Those women that are usurping authority by deliberately divorcing their husbands have no rewards in the kingdom to come. If the wife has maligned her husband to get a divorce or vice versa then that person could potentially be ejected from the kingdom and be thrown out and not be saved so slander (evil speech) is out. Going to church and singing a few nice hymns is not going to help either party.

The ones that do make it into the kingdom will not have any position of authority if the divorce was based on a flawed reason and there will even be marriages in the kingdom so what God does with these women or men will be revealed to us in due course. An argument or a fight over food or money is not a reason to divorce your spouse but separation is allowed <u>until</u> reconciliation if there is a valid reason such as the husband drinks too much and is drunk all the time or he abuses the wife physically then certainly an unrepentant husband gives the wife full reason for a divorce.

In a scenario where a wife demands an unreasonable divorce even if the husband has not been unfaithful is illegal according to the Torah. Sadly such men or women can never receive increases in this life or the next. They lose their rewards and that will be hard to swallow in the world to come. Many of these people will be slaves during the kingdom because they refused to obey the Father's Torah. Many of these will be evicted from the kingdom for lashon hara (evil speech).

### Divorce laws in the Torah

We will look at the different scenarios but first let us see if a divorce is at all possible.

> **Deut 22:13-21** "When any man takes a wife, and shall go in to her, and shall hate her, (14) and shall make abusive charges against her and bring an evil name on her and say, 'I took this woman, and when I came to her I did not find her a maiden,' (15) then the father and mother of the young woman shall take and bring out the proof of the girl's maidenhood to the elders of the city at the gate. (16) "And the girl's father shall say to the elders, 'I gave my daughter to this man as wife, and he hates her. (17) 'And see, he has made abusive charges against her, saying, "I did not find your daughter a maiden," and yet these are the proofs of my daughter's maidenhood.' And they shall spread the garment before the elders of the city. (18) "And the elders of that city shall take that man and punish him, (19) and fine him one hundred pieces of silver and give them to the father of the young woman, because he has brought an evil name on a maiden of Y'sra'el. And she is to be his wife, he is not allowed to put

her away all his days. (20) "But if the matter is true, that the girl was not found a maiden, (21) then they shall bring out the girl to the door of her father's house, and the men of her city shall stone her to death with stones, **because she has done wickedness in Y'sra'el, to <u>whore</u> in her father's house**. Thus you shall purge the evil from your midst.

בישראל לזנות בית אביה

B'Y'sra'el L'zanot Bayit Abe-ah.

The important Hebrew words to note she **played a whore in Y'sra'el in her father's house**.

We can see that a divorce was made possible in a scenario in what we term FRAUD. This happened while the girl was **in her father's house**. Note it is cutting of the Contract and not a paper divorce as we understand it. Most of our societies today are built on paganism not biblical laws so let's get that straight. Just because they have culled some laws from the Bible to use in their pagan systems we cannot say they are obeying or built on Bible laws that is a mistake that many believers make. Certainly what the governments have sowed they are reaping now.

If a girl has slept with someone and betrothed to another this was/is according to Torah a capital crime then she will not bleed on the first night and the man she married to finds out about it would create a big issue and it would be a problem for the man of course and for the girl. I will point out that sometimes in some exceptional circumstances a girl's hymen may dissolve without sexual contact for many reasons in which case a girl may not bleed which does not mean that she has been unfaithful but that does not preclude the man suspecting her of Fraud still.

If the husband hates his wife for no apparent reason the Torah mandates that he could be fined and not allowed to put his wife away for life and but if the matter was true then the girl could be stoned outside her father's house which would have become a public disgrace for the family.  So we need to understand that this would be for a <u>man</u> who hated his wife without a reason, a selfish cruel man, it is not nice for a man to fall this low towards the one he claims to love or have loved!  I will point out that though the Torah gave one injunction for divorce but the leading two rabbinic schools before Yahushua allowed divorces on various other grounds one of which believe it or not was bad cooking.

YHWH's provision was not to have rampant divorce but he provided provision for the <u>hatred</u> that ensued in the marriage because of the man.  Technically this law is to deal with the hatred of a man who cannot control his passion so if to be blunt it is to deal with a man from being cruel to his wife. I will also suggest that if a man is cruel to his wife during the marriage even in later years such as physical abuse she can legitimately enter a divorce plea if he is unwilling to repent of his bad behavior to his wife.

So the precursor for divorce is **Fraud** due to whoring/adultery <u>before</u> departure of the girl.  Please note biblical marriage was a betrothal and after this it was simply departure of the girl at a time when the father of the bridegroom decides to send his son to collect the bride.  The same analogy applies to us waiting for our Bridegroom Melek Yahushua.  In Muslim lands this is still practiced where a girl is wed in her father's house but the departure does not occur until an agreed time later such as one year or two years or even several years depending on the girl's age.  In Y'sra'el it was determined by the father of the bridegroom usually up to one year to two years.

One must understand that FRAUD can apply to either party in so far as a man can lie to a woman and later turn out to be a thief and scoundrel and she can get an annulment or divorce certificate called a "Get" by Rabbis so this is not a one sided law.  The Torah laws are very fair and just. Sadly most Christians are not taught these but they still apply as much today as yesterday.  We will look at other reasons and if they are viable.  So what happens if the woman is found to be whoring in ancient times, the result sadly was not

DIVORCE on demand but DEATH OF THE WOMAN and it was immediate and no Betty was not on death row for ten years while the husband holds on or Tim is on death row while Betty waits and endures the trauma for ten years. Y'sra'el did not have huge complexes for prisons but a ward where some guards would hold the culprit and justice would be very swift. The West unfortunately comes nowhere near the justice standards of Torah provisions. Y'sra'el did not feed the criminals on Tax payer's dollars with cable TV, games, education for five years before deciding their fate. Enter the ridiculous prison culture of the West.

Even in Islam's sha'ria laws come close to Y'sra'el's swift justice system in swiftness to execute someone but not to the justice standards of the Torah as the law in Islam is implemented without due diligence, witnesses and regards for the person on trial. Many times the culprits get away because of connections who they know and the innocent party gets executed instead. This would NEVER happen in Y'sra'el.

However crime figures in a pure Islamic state like Saudi Arabia are far lower than most Western nations. People can leave their shops and go to prayers without worrying about theft but try to leave your tills in Tesco's and Wal-Mart and you will come back to an empty store with thieves galore carrying TVs and food away. The cameras will catch people who are shoplifting for sure but because of the lack of capital punishment and its swiftness of justice it's a happy day for the thieves in Western lands carrying TVs, fridges, DVD players and the sort.

So both systems the Islamic and the Western lack with what God had given us to do. On comparison the Western system seems better/fairer but actually it is worse than the Islamic system because if you cannot pay for a good lawyer the chances of you getting true justice is fairly remote as the ones who can afford the better lawyers will get the better justice too. In other words how much cash you have determines your justice.

Now coming back to Betty you can see is it right that a life should be wasted like this because of a mistake committed and if the one committing the mistake realizes her fault and is repentant?

Would you want this for the one you took an oath with to love and to cherish to be dead?

The same law though misunderstood by many so called experts is also found in Deut 24:1-4.

Please note this is a complete paragraph from verses one to four and don't go by how it is split up in the KJV as it is not one verse in fact the Hebrew thought is 4 verses altogether correctly illustrated in the HTHS Bible.

> **Deut 24:1-4** When a man has taken a wife, and married her, and it come to pass that she find no favour in his eyes, because he has found some uncleanness in her: then let him write her a bill of divorcement, and give it in her hand, and send her out of his Beyth (house). **2** And when she is departed out of his Beyth (house), she may go and be another man's wife. **3** And if the latter husband hates her as well, and writes her a bill of divorcement, and gives it in her hand, and sends her out of his Beyth (house); or if the latter husband die, which took her to be his wife; **4** Her former husband, who sent her away, may not take her again to be his wife, after that she is ritually impure; for that is abomination before YHWH and You shall not cause the land to transgression, which YHWH Your POWER gives you for an inheritance.

The Hebrew word Ervah Dvar means some sexual impropriety such as a past affair or something similar. It can also be whoring.

The word for "favour" in verse one is chen and means "favour", "grace", "elegance" and "acceptance". When a husband finds out his wife had slept with someone before she married to him he becomes angry and thus has no more <u>favour</u> or <u>elegance</u> or <u>charm</u> for his wife. Sadly this happens a lot in Eastern Cultures and men can become very cruel to their wives, I have seen this first hand in Pakistan where Muslims can even kill their wives for this type of thing and this can create life long feuds. In Y'sra'el God allowed a hot headed man to cool himself down therefore a provision was made that if proven did not lead to divorce as most think but the DEATH OF THE WOMAN. Life is precious so we must think is this what we want for the sake of our hatred to kill someone else! If it takes someone else's death that you thought you loved to pacify your anger then I must say something is not right with this type of man.

It is again provision for what to do when a husband has lost his love for his wife and is burning with the passion of hatred. Many people discover the divorce law here but what I found upon God showing me here is how to deal with the uncleanness that a husband has found in his wife or has been made known to him after the marriage has consummated. To me this is not dealing with **divorce at all** as we all thought but the same principle as in Deut 22:13 where a husband finds no favour for his wife and could not love her any longer, started hating his wife and here also the idea is one husband whose heart has become hard and has also lost favour so he puts his wife away quietly rather than the public fanfare.

Have you ever wondered when the Pharisees came to Melek Yahushua in Matthew chapter 5, why didn't the Messiah simply quote Deut 24:1 and say go and be done with it?

> **Mat 19:5** And said, for this cause shall a man leave Ab and eem (mother), and shall cleave to his wife: and the two shall be one flesh?

If one understands this then why did the Messiah quote the passage from creation? This is because there was no **provision for divorce** but how to deal **with the hatred** that occurs either in a male or female when one loses favour for the other.

Hence why the Messiah said Moses did it for *the hardness of men's hearts* or women's for that matter.

> **Mat 19:8** He said to them, Musa because of the hardness of your hearts allowed you to put away your wives:[4] but from the beginning it was not so.

The provision was made not because it was right but because of men's hearts, it was not divorce if proven but DEATH. If a man sent his wife away quietly it was accepted that a man was hard hearted and could not bear with his wife. This actually occurred with Joseph too in the Renewed Contract when he knew his wife was with child, he was a right-ruling man and decided to put his wife away quietly but God told him not to as she was conceived with child through the Father in heavens and the Ruach Ha Kadosh (Holy Spirit).

> **Mat 1:19** Then Joseph her husband, being a just man, and not willing to make her a public example, was minded to put her away privily.

Question) What if my wife to be has already had sexual contact with someone before marriage and has told me that this happened then what?

Answer) We are Y'sra'elites and not heathens and do not behave as the nations do so MERCY and JUSTICE are our highest calling. A lot of us talk about it but sadly few really practice it. In this case you can marry the girl and the matter is closed as she is faithful to you as your wife there is no concern and you are not allowed to beat her up over it figuratively speaking for the rest of her life. If you cannot marry this girl or just because you found this out and it has hurt your feelings then it would be better that you would tell her at the point of finding out before marriage and drop the relationship rather than use this as an excuse to divorce her later to bring disgrace to yourself from God and disappointment and disrespect to her and her household. An unmarried girl is allowed to be another man's concubine or wife which after a divorce or breakup of a concubine relationship she is allowed to marry any Y'sra'elite. The only one forbidden to marry a non-virgin was the High Priest.

---

[4] The word is plural because we are allowed to have plural marriages as our lifestyle.

Since you cannot be the High Priest as Melek Yahushua stands in place for it then it does not affect you.

## What if there is no shedding of blood?

This does not mean that the marriage Contract does not stand because there is no shedding of blood (breaking of the hymen), the marital commitment still stands for each party since the witness is the God of Y'sra'el, who lives and never dies. We must know what we are entering is serious business and not a game. And a threefold cord is not quickly broken. (Ecc 4:12)

## What about the Messiah's words that you <u>can</u> put away your wife?

People who want to divorce usually read divorce into this but the Messiah Yahushua confirmed what the terms of the Deuteronomy 22:13-21 stipulations were if we are careful to read them.

> **Mat 5:32** But I say to you, that whosoever shall put away his wife, unless for the cause of whoring, causes her to commit adultery and whosoever shall marry her that is undivorced[5] commits adultery.

When the Messiah said "it has been said" He was not referring to Torah principles but to the ideas of Pharisees and Sadducees of marriage and divorce but

---

[5] Our view in the footnote is confirmed in the Aramaic Khabouris which says 'and whosoever taketh her who is sent away, committeth adultery.' The Peshitta Aramaic has undivorced. A divorced or put away woman cannot remarry if that marriage was broken for any frivolous reason such as bad cooking or she swore at me that would be considered a wrongful divorce. Marriage is a contract for life until the husband's death, and you would have to have your wife stoned to death for adultery so it is not divorce but death. However a marriage can be dissolved on various grounds for injustice by the Rebbim and the woman is allowed to remarry. Usually it is better to apply the injunction of Fraud in Deut 22:13-21. The marriage if not annulled then she is technically still married in the shamayim hence Yahushua is right and everyone else wrong!!! An injunction can be made by Rebbim where there are special circumstances to allow for divorce and remarriage this is within halacha, which would allow the woman to remarry.

He also quoted what Moses wrote given of course by The Messiah Himself on Mount Sinai. The Messiah suggested "**whoring**" not Adultery although it could qualify for both physical and spiritual adultery and even idolatry.

If you check the Hebrew, Melek Yahushua used the same Hebrew words found in Deuteronomy 22:21 L' Zanot, He did not connect this with Deuteronomy 24:1 but with Deuteronomy 22:21 and that is significantly important because He was making the connection with fraud and not just willful divorce as had started to happen in the first century Y'sra'eli society.

When does whoring occur?

Whoring occurs when a woman before her marriage goes and sleeps with different men who she does not intend to marry. Can she commit adultery after marriage? Yes, because if she is betrothed and before the departure to her husband's home sleeps around then yes she is whoring, while being married and has actually committed adultery, which was/is a serious transgression.

## The matter is not adultery as we all thought but uncleanness

We can see that the matter still related to FRAUD. If the husband found out in the marriage that his wife had been unclean or irresponsible in her past before being married to him then he could do the same thing as Deuteronomy 22-13-21 suggests but you may ask how come the matter in the previous scriptures was one of putting away and being public about it while here it is not public and no stoning was involved.

This is because the matter is one of Mercy and Justice. In the discourse of Deuteronomy 22:13-21 situation the husband being unjust made his wife's matter public and brought open shame to the whole family, while in Deuteronomy 24:1-4 the husband does not want to bring open shame to his wife and privately divorces her meaning he is a bit more gracious but not gracious enough to forgive the wife and simply accept bygones as bygones and live with her in love and harmony that is if the wife also wants to live in harmony.

In my opinion YHWH allowed the following three options:

1 Mercy
2 Forgiveness
3 putting her away if her past affair bothers you but no divorce as our current society model has established both with unrighteous and unjust laws. However I agree that some of the injunction of the Rabbis were correct to prevent abuse and injustice.

If the man cannot exercise his mercy and justice to accept the fact that what happened in the woman's past was something in her past and not present and that it should not be dwelt on. Forgiveness is the order of the day.

How about if you commit a sin and the penalty we know is death (Ezek 18:4) then what if I told you that you must die no matter what? Would you be happy that there is no way out? Hence why we know the Messiah made a way out for us because we were all destined to die otherwise but because of Him we live.

We needed a way out and it was provided by the Father in heaven through His Son. On either part of the husband or wife they MUST be willing to forgive the other party in a dispute else it is openly shameful to both families to carry out a public divorce since even God does not approve of a divorce as we all traditionally thought because it will either lead to stoning of the woman or her being married to you forever. The putting away privately is a more humane option in premarital sex pure and simple but not a **ground** for divorce.

My question is this that the second most important commandment is to love your neighbour as yourself Lev 19:18 and Matt 22:39 so if you are to love your neighbour then why can't you love your spouse and forgive the past or present circumstance that is hounding you? Why would you want to publicly humiliate your wife or husband for that matter? This is not a right-ruling thing to do and would bring shame upon the whole assembly of Y'sra'el and God never approves of such matters no matter who the guilty party is.

Beware Christianity and Torah followers God does not love slanderers, they will not enter the Kingdom unless they have repented and asked for forgiveness and received forgiveness from the one they slandered!!!

This is why He asked to put this behind Y'sra'el and remove it by death. The marital Contract is until DEATH.

If a wife has dealt with her husband treacherously or vice versa in a matter concerning adultery or non-adulterous matter, could even be for a household dispute or in a dispute where a religious or non religious matter is not shared between one spouse then this thing is most shameful and will bring reproach on both parties and whoever has brought this shame will have to suffer the consequences and lose rewards and a special place in the kingdom to come.

Just because the husband or wife have the support of many people does not make the action right in the Father's eyes. The wife or husband the guilty party may or may not lose their salvation depending on the gravity of the matter but they will certainly lose their rewards and any authority they were to possess in the coming kingdom. I ask is it worth it for the sake of this short life? A wife could publicly slander her husband and any parties that are involved in doing likewise will all have to answer for their rebellion in front of the King one day or did you think that all is well, just go to Church on Sunday, sing a few hymns, have cup of tea but its ok to slander? No, nothing escapes the King's attention and is meticulously recorded by the angels appointed to you for judgment day. WHEN BOOKS ARE OPENED YOU WILL BE FOUND WANTING AND GUILTY SO THINK THROUGH PRAYERFULLY OF ALL YOUR ACTIONS PLEASE FOR YOUR own SAKE.

The cruelest thing to do is to publicly slander your husband or wife showing complete lack of mercy or justice even if he or she is guilty. **YES EVEN IF HE/SHE IS GUILTY IT DOES NOT MAKE IT RIGHT.** Anyone acting in this fashion has got a big thing coming and prepare for Day of Judgment because what you have sown you will definitely reap **IN THIS LIFE** and the next. Some of you will be evicted from the kingdom for this type of behavior.

> **Job 4:8** (KJV) Even as I have seen, they that plow iniquity, and sow wickedness, reap the same. (9) By the blast of God they perish, and by the breath of his nostrils are they consumed.

What do you think that Melek Yahushua was publicly flogged spat upon and shouted at, did it make it right for Him to have these beatings considering He was innocent? Do you think in the world to come would those spitting on his face and lashing him will get a reward in the kingdom perhaps because Melek Yahushua had to die? The wicked will get their just punishment like Judah Iscariot. Just because he was a disciple was it right that he sold his Rabbi for thirty pieces of silver? Sadly some in churches will not be able to enter the kingdom because of their unjust behavior in this world so be careful how you treat others! Melek Yahushua's death and resurrection is not a license for sin as many have made it to be.

If you have a problem with any teachings in the bible and you make it your mission to slander God's appointed people or your spouse then you will have to pay the price as long as that brother or sister is holding to a Torah precept that is true such as had happened with some recently believing in Torah polygamy. This is Torah Truth and no amount of Church legislation is going to remove what the Father has clearly allowed in His perfect will. Hellenist scholars are not going to defeat sound Hebrew biblical teaching and the followers of that teaching.

I speak from experience don't slander your spouse, because slandering is a serious transgression that can keep you out of the kingdom. Hold your mouth and keep peace, YHWH will reward you for it. A wife slandering her spouse or vice versa does not make these actions just and right even if your spouse has done something wrong because love covers a multitude of sins.

Would that make an ensuing divorce on demand right? To many Christians yes but to us Y'sra'elites no, it remains to be a sin and the woman is committing sin and the martial Contract cannot end without death, the piece of paper a woman is attempting to receive from courts is meaningless and has no authority in heaven unless the husband releases her by his own free will. No amount of public slander against the head of the house (husband) is the right-ruling or merciful thing to do. What should have been done in any difficult situation is petition to seek the Father's will in the matter if it is His will for that marriage and not public slander. No Y'sra'elite woman was ever glorified in scriptures for doing as this.

**Those that tell you divorce is OK ask them to show you a public divorce in the bible. You won't find one.**

The most hated text by women in the West!

The woman was created for man and not man for woman hence why the man has to die to terminate the Contract. I know many Rabbi's would disagree with this but I stand corrected with Rabbi Yahushua who said both were created as one flesh and let no man separate what Elohim has put together.

Some ladies file a divorce for such matters and yet scripture does not allow divorce for those matters but this is the reality that we have to bear for living in the West where the women are simply out of control and think they are being holy and fighting a holy jihad against the polygamist belief but actually they are acting in the spirit of Lilith and Jezebel and for every sin there will be a consequence and a repercussion that they will have to bear both here and in the world to come. (A divorce is allowed for unjust husband or unjust wife or such as cruelty or violation of the contract) Be warned in the end they have a lot more to lose than to gain I assure you of this. Unrighteous behavior can never be given rewards and a pat on the back.

God caused the <u>first</u> woman to become a demoness and the second woman pains upon giving birth also ousted from the Garden with Adam for her disobedience for the rest of her days and ALL women today are still bearing the brunt of it today and so are the men even though Melek Yahushua died and rose again that curse remains. Chava (Eve) usurped Adam's authority to eat the fruit and on top of that fed it back to him. The moral of the story is do not listen to a woman in matters of God because the man has already been instructed, obey God's voice. This is not about putting women down, no not at all but faithful management of God's estate so women are not put down and kept in check and loved correctly. If Abraham had asked Sarah's advise to sacrifice his son Sarah would have objected and could even have called Abraham a lunatic for even suggesting something like this but he was a wise man who did not tell Sarah what he was about to do in order to protect her. Exercise wisdom in all matters and don't say God did not tell you this. Ask God to show you if He has spoken what is the right thing to do.

Using the standard of mercy and justice the matter must be committed to YHWH to exercise justice and right-ruling rather than hatred, slander and strife is the wrong thing to do. We have to accept the fact that someone's spouse may not share a Torah belief nor what God has shown a husband and that person is to remain quite knowing God is equitable and His throne rests on Justice and right-ruling (Ps 89:14) and will vindicate that person over time. He should never be bitter and do not fall down low to backstab other people because I know God can pay back and do <u>not</u> go all out to destroy your wife or husband this is the most wicked action, avoid it at all cost. I am not writing this from just reading the bible but personal experience, I know the pain and anguish and it is difficult when it happens to you but it is necessary and prudent to endure for His sake. Life does not end here after thirty or forty years but think of the Olam Haba (the world to come). You will be rewarded, while the other person will have to stand with a shamed face, to face the consequences of that action in front of YHWH the just and true God.

When you marry a person you usually marry for love at least in the west but in the east we have arranged marriages therefore one thing needs to be understood that a wife is the mirror of a man and reflects him. What you prophesy to her she will only give it back to you multiplied. If you call her stupid she will give you back a stupid person. You prophesied bad things to her so you receive the same, remember the mirror.

You are the sun and she is the moon, therefore she is a reflection of your light. If your light is defective and if she complains this then indicates that there is something you need to fix in yourself. Go fix whatever is wrong with you and it will fix her automatically. Do not criticize your wife but if you must do it then give her loving guidance if you feel she has to be told, do it politely without attacking her character, the more you criticize her. the more she amplifies it back to you remember she is also a sounding board. You give her something she simply amplifies it and gives it back to you. So in principle never criticize her and be cautioned so you know how to behave towards her. If she does not do the ironing correctly then you can guide her by doing it yourself this way you negate the criticism aspect, you can lovingly show her honey this is how I would iron the shirt and demonstrate it. If she made bad cooking then you can demonstrate to her by telling her honey next time I would like to cook while you watch that way you may learn some new techniques in cooking.

If the food got burnt no problem just take it easy and tell her not to worry the burnt food can go in the bin, ask her that you may order a take away dish so that she can rest her mind without worrying over re-cooking. Make it easy for her and adapt to the situation at hand. Do not sweat over little things and blow them up to crisis point. Let it go and be calm about it. It may also be that you are rushing her so much that in a hurry she made mistakes so the problem once again is in you to fix in yourself.

If she is your flesh would you stand in front of the mirror daily and curse yourself? Would you say to yourself I hate you, I don't like the way you cook, I don't like the way you iron my clothes. If you do then its time to change and look at your own behavior first. Fix yourself and she will be fixed automatically. You need to pay homage to YHWH and repent first and the problem will be resolved. Ask YHWH to show you why things are not working so that you have more awareness of the problems in yourself.

> **Psalm 103:6** YHWH executes right-rule and judgment for all that are oppressed.

I know it's easy to criticize and slander spouses to friends, relatives or even on the internet if you want to divorce your wife/husband. It happened to me too but we must keep serving the Father faithfully awaiting His justice and right-ruling. Do not be ashamed about it even though many people may be against you for a Torah truth, it is highly likely that this was a trial for your life and hopefully many others would learn important scriptural lessons from this. Always Stand firm for truth and do not sway because you received persecution to strengthen your character its good for you. Believe me you come out a stronger man.

We are not to take justice in our own hands but we are to act justly there is a huge difference. One's pain is many others gain. Melek Yahushua's death was our gain, remember the model. The one just died for All the unjust of Y'sra'el to pay for their transgressions.

> **John 15:13** Greater love hath no man than this that a man lay down his life for his friends.

Is your spouse not your friend to suffer for and would you be willing to lay down your life for her/him or do you want to publicly slander her/him? Love requires a sacrifice and is not determined by our financial worth our ego or pride.

Esteem be to God because I know many prophets in Y'sra'el suffered for YHWH's commandments when others around them refused to believe them. Moses the greatest prophet ever born is our best example who had to deal with Korah's rebellion his half brother and his own elder brother and his sister turning against him in rebellion that saw Miriam becoming leprous. If a man like Moses who spoke to God face to face was not spared then what are we but dust and no comparison? Our persecution is nothing in such matters because none of us have seen God as Moses did. Honestly our pain is water on a camel's back. I know we have many failings and do things wrong at times but I petition to the Most High that we will learn humility and to give Him esteem in all our situations.

Today its quite hip fashion for both men and women to refuse to agree with God's words and rather breach the Contract of marriage altogether.

If a wife or husband is put in such a position this does not mean that just because a local or national court has given the petitioner the divorce certificate therefore it is acceptable in God's sight unless it is a GET because it is NEVER acceptable and the wife in such a position would remain the wife of that husband by the Torah only if she married under the Torah but if she did not marry under the Torah then she was nothing more than in a human contract a type of concubine and therefore has the right to separate take a divorce and leave quietly.

She will get a double marriage if she looks to remarry without a GET and that is if she in the first place married with a ketubah. So be careful as all worldly contracts are not seen in the eyes of God as the same. As I stated unless the first husband has legally and without coercion happily released her only then is she able to go away and remarry without the consequence of adultery in a Torah marriage.

> **Mar 10:12** And if a woman shall put away her husband, and be married to another, she commits adultery.

You may ask what if the woman divorces her husband but does not remarry herself would then she still be committing adultery?

First of all no woman who divorces her husband in such an affair vows to live an ascetic life but even if she did she is still GUILTY OF THE SIN OF REBELLION which is the **sin of witchcraft**. God does not see asceticism as more pious and asceticism is **never** held above marriage. This idea only existed in the early Church fathers minds some of whom were hermits with a Greek idea of piety and nothing to do with the Y'sra'elite roots of our faith.

**Danger signs ahead**

While the rebellious wife thinks she is doing a jihad against her husband the foolishness is evident that her jihad is not against the husband at all but against God who is RESTORING all things back including Patriarchal marriages.

Question) What do I do with my wife who is rebellious and is physically abusing me?

Answer) If your wife is physically abusing you then this is really taking the cake. You have the eternal judge who will find a way to assist you so first and foremost make your request by petitions to Elohim.

The second thing is to talk to her and if she does not listen then you need to consider separating ASAP and be removed from the dwelling, you may be able to get a court order that refrains her from doing you harm and it could also be a man doing this to his wife but if there are children involved then the local government might throw you out instead. Ouch. Who said this world is just.

If you are getting a beating because of a disability and cannot defend yourself or some other reason like she is very strong not likely but it can happen. It might sound funny but it has happened to some. You can appeal to the local authorities but success is dependent on whose story they are likely to believe. Women always get the upper hand in the Greco/Roman western culture so your chances of success are very limited.

Failing to get a court order or the like you will have to remove yourself from the property and create distance between yourself and her. Divorce is not the solution for a rebellious wife but distance and petition to the Master of Heaven is. If she remains in rebellion then you can decide to terminate the marriage by divorce because of her uncleanness but a time of separation and petition to Melek Yahushua would help to decide the outcome.

Question) What do I do if I had divorced my husband and subsequently married and the divorce now realizing is illegal in God's eyes then what about the present marriage?

You are not going to like my answer but it is clear you are to separate in a dispute until such time as reconciliation. The wife cannot file for a divorce or remarry unless your husband divorced you before he married you meaning biblical betrothal and break up because you told him you had slept with someone else or he was defrauding you. However if you divorced your husband for any other reason there are several criteria which I cannot discuss all in here. The first one, are you or were you Y'sra'el meaning saved and in the covenants of God. If neither party was saved then your marriage was not recognized in God's sight hence if you subsequently remarried there is no sin provided you are in Messiah now and part of Y'sra'el. If you just did a worldly contract such as court marriage or even church marriage this is not counted or seen in the eyes of God so your divorce is fine and you are OK to remarry. Only if you had a ketubah you must get a GET (a divorce paper from a believing Rabbi).

Question) What if you were saved but ignorantly did this while your spouse was not saved?

This only matters if you got a Ketubah in your previous marriage and it's unlikely that you have hence you have no problem to remarry.

These are difficult issues with no yes and or no answer as there are many permutations to look through. In God's eyes you would be seen to be "whoring" with any other man after a marriage has broken unlawfully in His sight if a ketubah was made and you subsequently broke the marriage without a GET. The question is what is lawful and what is unlawful that is what we as teachers have to get right through Torah legislation. This has been debated for a very long time and I am certain it will continue to be debated until the Messiah returns.

**Ervat Devar on Deuteronomy 24:1**

> [1]We can see this pattern--which characterizes much of rabbinic action, or non-action, for many ensuing centuries--begin to emerge in an early rabbinic dispute between the schools of Hillel and Shammai (first century B.C.E.). Shammai, the strict constructionist of biblical law, maintained that the scriptural words *ervat davar* [meaning "some fault or indecency," which was the standard biblical grounds for divorce] meant, literally and exclusively, "adultery." Thus, a woman's infidelity was the only legitimate grounds for divorce. Hillel, known as a liberal because he generally interpreted Scripture more broadly, interpreted ervat davar as anything that was offensive to the husband. As in most disputes, rabbinic law followed Hillel.

Question) What if a wife defiled the marriage bed and slept with another man and committed adultery after the marriage?

This matter was hotly debated in the first century also between the school of Shammai and the school of Hillel. Shammai agreed divorce was only possible in adultery/uncleanness while Hillel said in any matter one could divorce the wife but Yahushua concluded that uncleanness/whoring would allow you to put your wife away if you could not forgive her or she did not seek forgiveness hence one could argue that this is uncleanness if not forgivable by the husband (remember the hard heart) could allow a divorce paper to be given but you have to learn to forgive if your wife is repentant else which court can you go to get her stoned to death? None for now until the third Temple and Messiah are back. Mercy and Justice must prevail. If the wife desires to be released then you have to release her through a Get which can be acquired from a Rabbi.

**Why would the disciples say "this is such a hard thing" if it was so easy to divorce one's spouse and walk away from the marriage?**

Let us see the admonition.

> **Mat 19:4** And he answered and said unto them, Have ye not read, that he which made them at the beginning made them **male and female**,

He quoted the verses from Genesis for creation to show a woman was created for the man meaning husband. Sorry wives you have to be submitted to your husband for life that is if he is a right-ruling Torah upholding man.

> **Mat 19:5** And said, for this cause shall a **man leave father and mother**, and shall **cleave to his wife**: and they twain shall be **one** flesh?

The man/woman (Husband/wife) is destined to be joined to each other in a sexual union to be completed as Akhad (A unity of two). A man can be Akhad with more than one wife but a wife cannot be Akhad with more than one man as scripture does not allow it just like the Messiah is Akhad with many of His brides. Allegorically each person is a bride but there is only ever ONE husband The Messiah. There is many to one relationship. Each Bride (believer) is Akhad with the Messiah (Bridegroom). A woman cannot be Akhad in polyandry (More than one husband) as mixing is forbidden in the Torah.

> **Mat 19:6** Wherefore they are no more twain, but one flesh. What therefore Elohim hath joined together, **let no man** (or ANY man) put asunder.

NO MAN ALSO MEANS NO JUDGE OF THE LAND HAS THE RIGHT TO BREAK A MARRIAGE CONTRACT, POLYGYNY OR NO POLYGYNY, FIGHT

OR NO FIGHT, ARUGMENT OR NO ARGUMENT, AGREEMENT OR DISAGREEMENT. A MARRIAGE CONTRACT IS ONLY <u>BREAKABLE</u> BY <u>DEATH</u>!

YHWH'S TORH RULES ETERNALLY – However an unjust husband or unjust wife can call in the divorce.

This is why in the husband hating the wife scenario if proven the wife had to die or the husband had to be fined and never to divorce his wife.

Melek Yahushua's Disciples even found the matter difficult to absorb but friends yes it is difficult I admit hence why we need to be careful with our actions and not willy nilly be divorcing if it can be avoided. We are real people with emotions and feelings and not furniture that can just be relocated and replaced from one house to the next.

If a spouse has put you in this situation then let God recompense her or him so in that case you are in no sin to remarry however your wife cannot unless you are dead or you have released her legally according to Torah by a Get provided your marriage was by a Ketubah (marriage contract) and if not then she can be released without one.

Question) What about Abraham asking his son Ishmael to divorce his first wife, didn't he command divorce?

> **Yashar 21:28-32** But she was beating her children in the tent, and she was cursing them, and she also cursed her husband Ishmael and reproached him, and Abraham heard the words of Ishmael's wife to her children, and he was very angry and displeased. 29 And Abraham called to the woman to come out to him from the tent, and the woman came and stood opposite to Abraham, for Abraham was still mounted upon the camel. 30 And Abraham said to Ishmael's wife, When thy husband Ishmael returneth home say these words to him, 31 A very old man from the land of the Philistines came hither to seek thee, and thus was his appearance and figure; I did not ask him who he

nd seeing thou wast not here he spoke
e and said, When Ishmael thy husband
eth tell him thus did this man say, When
omest home **put away this nail** of the tent
thou hast placed here, and place another
its stead. 32 And Abraham finished his
ctions to the woman, and he turned and
off on the camel homeward.

    Now the debate is whether this is a divorce or simply sending the wife back to her father's house for a fix up? I would suggest that this is not a divorce but simply sending the wife back home but again I know many Rabbis would see this as a divorce and a direct replacing of the wife.  I would personally tread on caution and take the least restrictive path because Moses did the same thing with Zipporah and she returned with her father later in the story.  So if it was a divorce then I would contend why did Zipporah return?  I know Western culture does not understand this because here people do not return to the father's house but the ladies go rent a place and start their life and start living with someone else.  They add relationship unto an existing relationship ending up in the adultery scenario.  Abraham did not command his son a divorce but send her back and fix up the nail, let the nail be polished and renewed.

    In Middle-Eastern culture such is not the case where the woman is dependent on the father and brothers so it is a different ball game altogether.  Yes she may not become a new nail but the nail will get polished and realize she made mistakes and may decide to repent else she will have to spend the rest of her days in her father's house and this still happens in many Muslims countries today.  However there is a second issue in with this where Abraham the Patriarch is the father of Ishmael and Ishmael had to obey the father so this explains his obedience to his Dad.  Remember the Ten Commandments divorce is not mentioned but obedience to the parents is.  Many Christians would do well to learn this.

    The third issue was that Ishmael's first wife was cursing her husband and had actually broken spiritual headship and this could be seen to be cursing God as the husband is directly the authority on the earth so in this case one could argue that she could be removed on the law of spiritual Zanah or spiritual idolatry safely hence why Abraham could have said to put her away. We are not told if she ever returned so to argue for divorce in the absence of this detail to me is conjecture while Moses' story proves this can happen, so to send off to the father a polish up and a return of the wife. This is a common practice in the eastern culture.

What did the Messiah mean?

> **Mat 5:32** But I say to you, that whosoever shall put away his wife, unless for the cause of whoring...

The two words used are:

The Greek word porneia G4202
[2]

**1)** To set free
**2)** To let go, dismiss, (to detain no longer)
**a)** A petitioner to whom liberty to depart is given by a decisive answer
**b)** To bid depart, send away
**3)** To let go free, release
**a)** A captive i.e. to loose his bonds and bid him depart, to give him liberty to depart
**b)** To acquit one accused of a crime and set him at liberty
**c)** Indulgently to grant a prisoner leave to depart
**d)** To release a debtor, i.e. not to press one's claim against him, to remit his debt
**4)** Used of divorce, to dismiss from the house, to repudiate. The wife of a Greek or Roman may divorce her husband.
**5)** To send one's self away, to depart

> **Mat 1:19** Then Yosef her husband, being a right-ruling man, and not willing to make her a public example, decided to put her away privately.

This is why Joseph a just man and not a hateful husband (Deut 22:13-21) was willing to put away his wife <u>quietly</u> thinking that he had found some uncleanness in his wife. Now in my opinion this is the ONLY case I see for putting your wife away and remember Joseph had NOT consummated the marriage so this was very early before the marriage bed had been even used. THE ISSUE AS I PROVE NOW IS OF FRAUD.

The Greek word moichao G3429

**1)** To have unlawful intercourse with another's wife, to commit adultery with[3]

Can you now see that the divorce that our King Messiah was stipulating was the same one that the book of Deuteronomy 22-13-21 mentions where uncleanness had to be found and not just anything e.g. the wife wants to divorce her husband because he believes in patriarchal marriage or the taking on of another wife? Clearly Yahushua showed that by doing the divorce on demand you are forcing your wife to lie down with another man and commit unlawful sex.

   As a Rabbi (teacher) my primary suggestion to the woman is to petition Master YHWH and seek the will of our Father in heaven and take action as directed, this will glorify Him even in your suffering. As a secondary solution if you think you cannot handle it at all I would suggest separation and divorce as a last resort only if the husband is unjust or cruel in some way.

   Your wife/husband if they are in adultery and in open rebellion then they have **breached the Contract** and this would be in my mind's eyes be a reasonable ground for a divorce in our time but the call has to be made with justice and mercy. It would only be right if your husband was given time and if he refused to repent. A certain time needs to be attached to the repentance, my suggestion is at least one year though even six months may be sufficient time to see if things become better or not.

Adultery should mean just that and not what the common term has come to mean in the Christian Church. A married man sleeping with a single woman is not adultery and not even fornication as that is a concubine relation since the single woman consented. This is not a ground for divorce

> **Exodus 22:16** "And if a man entices a virgin who is not betrothed, and lies with her, he shall surely pay the bride-price for her to be his wife.

This means the wife would not be able to force her hand and force a divorce. Sorry the Torah overrides you ladies.

If on the other hand He/She is willing to repent then forgiveness is paramount and MUST be given. You cannot withhold forgiveness and hope for you to be forgiven at the stake of Yahushua while having a hard and bitter heart toward this situation. Remember Justice and mercy are paramount and top priority in every believer's life. If the husband was NEVER wrong and you have realized you were wrong then you have to RETURN to your husband even if He has re-married or you have remarried, your marriage cannot stand because God allows biblical Patriarchal marriages and since you may be his first wife it is no problem as he has to give you the position back as before with full honour to restore you. Your subsequent marriage if you are a woman is nothing more than an adulterous affair and cannot stand. Don't you love the Torah it solves every problem of societal injustice. The truth shall really set you FREE.

Questions) What about if a man/woman married who were unbelievers and divorced.

Can such a woman remarry?

Answer) There is no Contract and there living together is just like common law marriage and not recognized in front of God. He does not recognize marriages made to heathen deities. There are many permutations of this so if you are in any of these situations you would have to write to me and ask for guidance to africanysrael@yahoo.com. The advice will be free.

**Scenario:**
A man clearly one day in prayer revealed by God to marry two women and the one woman was divorced but her situation was the one I mentioned above. Neither were believers in their marriage at the time of marriage but she became a believer later after her divorce so yes a non-believer can join into a martial Contract with a believer without any problems even if she was divorced as an unbeliever as long as the woman now submits to the God of Y'sra'el.

    I also came across the situation of Deuteronomy 22:13-21 and I was shown by God that as long as the woman has declared to the future believing husband that she had in the past made the mistake of sleeping with someone else in other words as a short term concubine by agreement, all boyfriend and girlfriend scenarios in the west are concubine contracts. The woman is allowed to marry a Hebrew believer without issue as long as the husband is happy that this had happened prior to his marriage.

Question) My husband beats me up black and blue and is on drugs are you saying I cannot divorce him?

Answer) Divorce is not your solution to the beating or abuse but you can separate from the abusive husband immediately until such time he repents and returns, give him time from six months to a year. If he does not repent then you are in your right to divorce him as he has breached the marital contract.

What if a woman cannot live with this situation?

> **Deut 21:18-21** If a man has a stubborn and rebellious son, which will not obey the voice of his father, or the voice of his mother, and that, when they have chastened him, will not listen to them: 19 Then shall his father and his mother lay hold on him, and bring him out to the elders of his city, and to the gate of his place; 20And they shall say to the elders of his city, This our son is stubborn and rebellious, he will not obey

our voice; he is a glutton, and a drunkard. 21 And all the men of his city shall stone him with Stones 10 that he dies: so shall You put evil away from among you; and all Y'sra'el shall hear, and fear.

In Y'sra'el if a son was unruly, drunkard then after warnings he could be brought before judges and would be stoned to death so there lies our precedence of unruly unrepentant people. Even if a son is fifty years old the parents remain the parents this is eastern culture reality of the Bible, first of all report the unruly son to the parents and if there are none then your congregation pastors or Rabbis should be able to help.

If all else fails then set before YHWH a time limit that you are willing to wait and if he has not repented and returned you can then decide what is the right thing to do but in this scenario again the provision is death not divorce but considering the rules of mercy and justice if you had children and had no support system then You should take a Get (biblical divorce) and do as you think is right with your life.

I went through a situation where a woman was beaten up black and blue and her husband was on drugs, the woman was very brave not to divorce the husband and the situation lasted about four years on and off beatings and I witnessed the bruising of the woman personally often times being there when the husband swore to the wife and cursed her and I would try to help them calm down. He was also unfaithful and sleeping with other women though probably not adulterous as the women were single. The situation could not be any worse at the time and I had a lot of compassion for the woman and the man for being on drugs the cause of his problems.

Some of you will be quick to cut the marriage and run for your lives but this woman had two children and did not want a divorce. Later her husband took counseling with her helping him and got rehabilitation and he got healed of his drug addiction completely and then out went the beating as well. The marriage was completely restored from disaster.

The woman is now happily married. This woman is a Muslim. I have never seen such resolve in a woman as much as this one and when I look at Christian ladies it shames me that they have no resolve even with the living God to wait but they rush for the divorce courts at a minute's notice and their mercy runs thin on the ground and usually the second husband they find turns out even worse.

Later then they decide that it was better to be with the first and want to go back but wrong churchy doctrine is what stops them going back misapplying scripture. Likely their second marriage is adulterous because the break of the first marriage is unwarranted and illegal according to scripture. No wonder the Messiah Yahushua said whosoever has ears listen. I never understood in all the years of faith why some Christians can be so <u>heartless</u> at times and so brutally merciless yet they received a bounty of mercy from the living God but where is their mercy when it comes to someone else being at their mercy?

> **Luke 17:4** (KJV) "And if he sins against you seven times in a day, and seven times in a day comes back to you, saying, 'I repent,' you shall forgive him."

I will emphasize also that forgiveness does not mean abandonment, since marriage is a Contract you cannot abandon your spouse or say you are forgiving them and still divorcing them because you cannot live with them. This is hypocrisy and would not be acceptable in God's court however in this world's court you can do as you please with plenty of other disobedient Christians egging you for support, but don't expect mercy when all you are willing to dish out is hatred hence you will receive the same back. What you sow you reap.

Question) My husband has been unfaithful and slept with other married women and has given me sexually transmitted diseases do I have the right to take divorce?

Answer) Life is precious and is to be guarded above all, if your husband has fallen into this kind of sin where he is not only adulterous but now has become a carrier for STD I would advise at first instance to separate from him and ask him or give him time to repent. If he refuses or is still continuing to live in sin then in that case if we were living in Y'sra'el with Torah rather than in the Diaspora he would be dead, killed by the judiciary with his adulterous women but for all practical purposes at least here in the Diaspora applying equal weights and measures you can divorce him for the sake of your life and of course the life of your children if you have any, I would be of the opinion that you are not under any sin as for that man is dead in your conscience since of his sin he refuses to repent pure and simple and you can safely remarry. Give him time perhaps six months of separation. If after the time no repentance is shown by him then go to a Rabbi and get the legal Get and then also you can do your local divorce courts for common law purposes.

Question) Why can't I have a divorce pure and simple?

Answer) For men God provided plural marriages so there should never be a need for a divorce or to put your wife away unless she is adulterous. Let me explain God set the law in Deuteronomy 21:10 that you were to take care of the 1$^{st}$ wife even if you took a second wife, now do you want to know why that was put there.

> **Exodus 21:10** If he takes another wife, he shall not diminish her food, her clothing, and her marriage rights.

In my understanding God never said why would you son want to take a 2$^{nd}$ wife but instead He knew through His perfect will that this was to happen as men are designed to have plural marriage, either they will do it according to the Torah and if you stop them then they will do it wrongly and some may likely have a genuine reason to marry a second/third wife for children but some may just want to do it for reasons such as I don't like my 1$^{st}$ wife so I must get another hence God made the law so that the 1$^{st}$ wife will not get abused and will always be the principle wife and have Rights for her children also. Some evil men who may try to divorce their 1ˢᵗ wife purely because they want to marry a second wife as they stopped loving the first wife so God ensured no DIVORCE and no evil occurs in Y'sra'el because the women were protected in Y'sra'el under God's Torah as the weaker vassal.

Let us see how this affects Y'sra'el and Y'sra'elites.

Let us take two Hebrew people and they marry, one then becomes disgruntled, let's assume it is the man since men are more prone to this behavior though women may also be but for this example I will choose a man to demonstrate the problem. He gets up one day and divorces his wife and sends her back to her father's house. Where else could she go? The people who live in the West are clueless on the hardships faced by divorced women in the Eastern cultures. Women are looked down and no one wants to remarry them, they are taunted and subjected to societal abuse, parental abuse, relative's abuse and worst strangers abuse, who may try to take advantage of them as they are most vulnerable. In a simple equation no husband and therefore no protection.

Now would the God of Y'sra'el want to leave His children out like that? You have to be wrong to think that He would. No, He wouldn't. He is our God of mercy and the God of ALL Y'sra'el He would never want to leave us in distress so He made sure the provisions were there for this abuse not to take place in the first place hence why we can also understand that Patriarchal marriages are His perfect will because it affords wives protection in the household though I know all may not choose this and prefer monogamy that is the men's choice. No this is not about a fallen world and an allowance as some Torah teachers suggest why because in the Millennium kingdom to come some men will have seven wives. I know Christians love to allegorize away everything but this is not allegory but a real reality like marriage is a real reality in the millennium and children would be born to the believers.

> **Isa 4:1** And in that day **seven women** shall take hold of one man, saying, We will eat our own

bread, and wear our own apparel: only let us be
called by thy name, to take away our reproach.

Now let's apply a harsher scenario. A Hebrew man
just divorces his wife for any reason and sends her out.
No other Hebrew man can marry her as she is divorced
unlawfully therefore causes adultery (Matt 5:32) then
where does this woman go for protection?

The only other people willing to marry Hebrew
women without caring about Torah or Messiah would
then be outside goyim (gentile/heathen) nations so what
do you think would then happen? She would join to a
heathen who worships a false god and then she ends
up with no salvation if she follows her new husband's
way. Is that a good thing?

Another man from the heathen clan could take her
and does the same thing to her. The poor woman is
lost for good. Remember none of her marriages to the
heathens is valid or a Contract because she is living in
complete and utter adultery and idolatry possibly even
worshipping false heathen gods as is her heathen
husband. No that is not a binding Contract as some
think between a false god and the two getting married
under him because the false god does not exist and you
cannot bind something with that which does not exist.
By the way this includes marriages made in Churches
under the name Jesus since that is not the name of
God. His name is YHWH. So if you call out in YHWH's
name and seal it in Yahushua's name then that is fine
but Churches do not do that hence their formed
marriage is also just a common law marriage and not
biblical.

> **Mal 2:16** For YHWH, the Elohim of Y'sra'el,
> says that he hates putting away: for one covers
> violence with his garment, says YHWH of hosts:
> therefore take heed to your ruach (spirit), that
> you deal not treacherously.

So if God hates divorce does that seem plausible to
you that He will allow you to divorce your wife for just
anything? We have shown that it is not so this is why

He enacted laws to protect all the commonwealth of Y'sra'el.

A Hebrew man taking one or more wives could decide to add widows to his household and that is fine too. This would be in mercy and justice and not as people think in sexual lust. However contrary to popular belief the real meaning of the word lust deliberately misconstrued in the bible is desire. A sexual desire is a healthy God given desire so if a man has a healthy desire he is in no sin to add on extra wives as long as he is able to support them financially.

Melek Dawud was a right-ruling man and he married Abigail (1 Sam 25:39) and it was in mercy and justice and even if King Dawud had sexual desire to do so there is no sin in it as he had many wives before he took her and he was able to afford his wives too. She was the widow of Nabal (1 Sam 25:3) who was an evil man so king Dawud certainly made a good husband to her.

We need to be careful because using our Western worldly standards we can apply the wrong idea on to what the Scriptures teach and end up completely being wrong. Petition to YHWH that He shows you His laws and gives you understanding of His laws because they are made in mercy and justice.

Question) What if the man lied and turned out to be someone else after marriage?

Answer) The same law in Deut 22:13-21 that applies to a woman can then also be reversed and used because Fraud had occurred, the man claiming to be one thing turned out to be someone else so that marriage can safely be voided and a Get (certificate of divorce) taken.

## **Oaths and Contracts**

Question) Can a wife in a marriage stipulate monogamous only relationship and make that binding?

Answer) This has been happening throughout history when women have done this but personally I neither agree with it nor would sign such an ketubah or marriage contract because to me it overrules God's provision for biblical polygamy and I would contend what if God instructed the man later to go get another wife then what are you going to do with the ketubah that says he can't. What if the woman withholds conjugal rights from the man and then tells him he cannot go get a second wife as he has signed a contract and she withholds marital relations with him? Then this in my mind creates room for injustice towards the husband and I am personally convicted that God's laws are above all and cannot be rescinded by man's laws so <u>no</u> I will never be seen signing such Ketubahs (marriage contracts). I know the Rabbis did in the past sign these so you will have to find a Rabbi who is willing to put pen to paper and be responsible for such a marriage not this one.

Question) What if a husband goes insane then should the wife still be bound to the husband?

Answer) The case has to be decided by Elders in the assembly if one exists or a knowledgeable Rabbi if this can happen since mercy and justice are our highest calling in Messiah I believe in such a case the woman can be released provided the woman sees fit to do such a thing and decides that since her husband is insane and in a mental institution that she sees no hope of him ever recovering. I would stipulate that a timeline be given such that allows room for the man's possible recovery before the divorce/re-marriage of the woman. I believe holding the woman bound to such a marriage creates lack of mercy because she does have the right to move on as she may have little children to feed if the situation is one of illness and hopelessness. However we must remember that when vows were taken both parties agreed that they would be together in sickness and in health. One has to then decide what that sickness is and what it means in the long term so as not to dishonour God and make the provision for the woman who may struggle on her own to feed the children.

Question) God divorced his wife the house of Y'sra'el and sent her away with a certificate (Isa 50:1) then retook Y'sra'el as a wife then why can't we?

Answer) I am afraid we cannot use this as precedence to break the law in Deuteronomy 24:1-4 that says a wife that is sent away and goes and marries another and even if her second or third husband dies cannot return. Unless you have the ability to die and resurrect yourself I would refrain from such an action. You are not Yahushua and the divorce in Scriptures is allegorically shown to be a case for the release of the wife after the death of Messiah. We know a wife can be released at the death of the husband according to Torah. Now the Messiah had the power to rise after death and then re-take His wife. You and me we do not have such powers so to me that law cannot be applied to mere humans.

So to sum up any human oath/contract that stipulates something that is intrinsically against YHWH's law at least in my opinion is not worth the paper it is written on unless it confirms a Torah precept and any such contracts are to be avoided. I know some Rabbi's would sign these contracts.

The case that Yahushua presented to His disciples was one where the Deut 22:-13-21 enactment would allow a marriage to dissolve because of Fraud. The issue was **whoring** and the requirement was either **public stoning** in front of the father's house or putting away your wife quietly. The question is that if you are a hateful husband and hate your wife then there is no central Beyth Deen (House of Judgment) in Y'sra'el today for believers where you can take your case and who is going to sanction for your wife to be stoned in front of your father's house and be killed? Practically that law cannot be enacted until a standing future 3$^{rd}$ Temple is here and Yahushua is back on the earth so in my opinion and knowledge that law is right now <u>suspended</u> but still very much valid as all the other capital laws in the Torah for punishment.

The option that you have thus is the second one where you can put your wife away quietly and not create a scene and yes you can do that provided there

is verifiably evidence or personal confession that Fraud had occurred or if your marriage is being terminated for another reason. Wouldn't you be more forgiving if your spouse confessed? I would appeal for MERCY and JUSTICE.
Melek Yahushua said the following:

> **Matthew 19:10** His disciples said to Him, "If such is the case of the man with his wife, it is better not to marry."

Melek Yahushua was not contradicting the laws of patriarchal marriage because Christians who lack Torah instruction take this to mean a man cannot have a second wife and that is adultery but this is not what Yahushua was saying at all. A man can have a second and even a third wife and it is not adultery provided he can keep all three provided for Exodus 21:10 and the number one takes precedence in inheritance and the rights of the children. The present model as stated earlier is one of Roman/Greco thinking and has nothing to do with the Biblical laws of relationship. Biblical monogamy is a valid choice of marriage but is one of a commitment of a lifetime and not for a season for six months, our people always started with monogamy but later switched to polygamy. They always started with one wife adding others later as the need was seen to place in the North and South of the country.

Yahushua set the precedence for the issue of Fraud (Whoring) you can put away your wife else you must stay put with your wife till your death that is the Contract agreement.

The disciples clearly a bit perturbed because it was the norm in the 1$^{st}$ century for many Hebrew people to divorce their wives if a man did not like her cooking hence now Yahushua corrected what man had corrupted. This was to protect the women. Sadly our culture is fully corrupted by Western Roman/Greek laws so **divorce on demand** exists to break families apart and no wonder England in Europe has the highest break up of marriages thanks to the corrupted minds of women and men of both believers and unbeliever alike both are bad as each other and I feel sorry for the children who needlessly suffer. There may be many other situations that need to be thought through and each one requires careful and prayerful thinking and certainly not rushing to the divorce courts.

Q) Can I divorce my wife if she is rebellious and wants to celebrate unclean church feasts?

A) If your spouse wants to celebrate unclean feasts the only loving thing you can do is to let her do that outside the home and petition to the Master for her but this does not command divorce. There is a headship issue and this can only be resolved over time. If you file for divorce you will stand guilty of treating the lesser vassal with dishonor. The other question is that she may not object to you keeping Torah which means you may have some semblance of peace. We are to pursue peace because increased are the peacemakers. Scripture does not say increased are the divorce makers.

Q) Can I divorce her if she is an unbeliever?

A) The admonition is to live in peace if she wishes to dwell with you.

The word that is used in Matthew 5:32 for divorce.

> **Mat 5:32** "But I say to you that whoever puts away [apoluo] his wife, except for the **matter of whoring**,[1] makes her commit adultery.

apoluo – Strong's G630 To release or to put away

*Also note the word for "uncleanness" is the word which means if she is "whoring" remember what I said about Deuteronomy 22:13-21 the situation is the same. This is the situation for whoring not a marriage where she was with the man for say two years then decided to divorce him or other way around.*

The word for "whoring" or as some Bible translators have used the word "fornication" although "whoring" is the correct one. The Greek word is porneia, this is deliberately twisting and mistranslation of Scripture.

*Without me even saying anything you would know what Porneia means. It is the Strongs G4203; meaning "harlotry" (including adultery and incest); "figuratively idolatry."*

Question) God divorced his wife so surely since He could divorce His northern wife why can't I?

Answer) God divorced Northern Y'sra'el, issued her a certificate of divorce, she went away whoring with other gods and became paganised. The present state in many assemblies. The Messiah then died because she would be free (Deut 24: and He husband could retake her back if she subsequently does not remarry and has fixed herself. Now are you able to die and rise up to take back your wife? If not then don't try this exercise as it will be foolish. This was to show the power the Messiah has to redeem the unfaithful wife whom He could die and be raised for but we have no personal powers to do that. Once we are dead we have no power to raise ourselves but only God can raise us and we have to wait until the coming of Messiah.

Question) Judah divorced his wives in Babylon when Ezra spoke to them so surely divorce was allowed otherwise how could Judah do this?

> **Ezra 10:19** And they gave their promise that they would put away their wives; and being guilty, they presented a ram of the flock as their trespass offering.

Answer) The issue in Babylon was not one of leaving your faithful Contract wife but one of paganism. You were not allowed to take a pagan/foreign wife outside Y'sra'el or one who rejected the God of Y'sra'el. Efrayim had transgressed by doing exactly this so they were living in rebellion to God's laws hence this was not a divorce in the normal sense as most people think. Do not use this as your tool for divorce. A divorce in scripture technically is a cutting, meaning separation it is not as many people have made it today such as handing a piece of paper and going sleeping with another man by cutting another Contract because a woman CANNOT cut two CONTRACTS until one is terminated. THIS IS WHORING. Women who are doing this are committing WHORING and are living in Sin.

There is no place for WHORES in the kingdom. Sorry I did not make these laws YHWH did.

> **Ezra 10:18** And among the sons of the priests who had taken **pagan wives** the following were found of the sons of Jeshua the son of Jozadak, and his brothers: Maaseiah, Eliezer, Jarib, and Gedaliah.

Please note why the writer keeps mentioning the word pagan. This was an unrighteous union. This was forbidden in Torah Deut 7:3. These were even priests who could only take Y'sra'elite virgin women but they were also guilty of violating the Contract.

Friends I know what the deal is, I have been through it so I write from personal trials and experience I received and what God has showed me and taught me so do not be hasty and do not be judgmental to axe your marriage you are NOT allowed to do this unless you have scriptural reasons to do so. Be careful of what words you use because the tongue is the member that is hard to control and one which will cause the most damage. We are NEVER to remove our covenantal wife or deal with her treacherously. I pray that the advice is heeded by all believers in Messiah.

## Additional comments on fornication and a license

The marriage contact is a three part contract between the man, woman and state known as an adhesion contract which favors the state.

By the way the Most High is never party to this contract.

So according to black's law when you marry or ask for a marriage contract from the state you are asking permission to carry out an unlawful act that the State itself many years prior had deemed unlawful and only made it lawful to make money and to entrap you and your future offspring. The word "License" means a revocable permission to commit some act that would otherwise be unlawful. (Blacks Law 7th Ed)

By doing this you are giving your State or government power over your marriage and your offspring so they can act at any time to legally seize your children or any other undue demand upon you through the act of getting a marriage license. The entire fault lies with you that you were deceived into acquiring a license that you need not have had in the first place. When your children are born they belong to the State through the solemnization of the Birth Certificate scam.

When Pastors and Bishops marry people in Churches they do so under State authority and not the authority of the Most High El. They are in treason to YHWH and in fellowship with Satan and the State that do not OBEY the Torah.

The State doctrine of Parens Patriae is applied;

## Parens Patriae

[Latin, Parent of the country.] *A doctrine that grants the inherent power and authority of the state to protect persons* [6]*who are legally unable to act on their own behalf.*

The *parens patriae* doctrine has its roots in English Common Law. In feudal times various obligations and powers, collectively referred to as the "royal prerogative," were reserved to the king. The king exercised these functions in his role of father of the country.

In the United States, the *parens patriae* doctrine has had its greatest application in the treatment of children, mentally ill persons, and other individuals who are legally incompetent to manage their affairs. The state is the supreme guardian of all children within its jurisdiction, and state courts have the inherent power to intervene to protect the best interests of children whose

---

[6] http://legal-dictionary.thefreedictionary.com

welfare is jeopardized by controversies between parents. This inherent power is generally supplemented by legislative acts that define the scope of child protection in a state.

The state, acting as *parens patriae*, can make decisions regarding mental health treatment on behalf of one who is mentally incompetent to make the decision on his or her own behalf, but the extent of the state's intrusion is limited to reasonable and necessary treatment.

The doctrine of *parens patriae* has been expanded in the United States to permit the attorney general of a state to commence litigation for the benefit of state residents for federal antitrust violations (15 U.S.C.A. § 15c). This authority is intended to further the public trust, safeguard the general and economic welfare of a state's residents, protect residents from illegal practices, and assure that the benefits of federal law are not denied to the general population.

States may also invoke *parens patriae* to protect interests such as the health, comfort, and welfare of the people, interstate Water Rights, and the general economy of the state. For a state to have standing to sue under the doctrine, it must be more than a nominal party without a real interest of its own and must articulate an interest apart from the interests of particular private parties.

**License**

**Modern definition**
*The permission granted by competent authority to exercise a certain privilege that, without such authorization, would constitute an illegal act,*
*a* Trespass *or a* TORT. *The certificate or the document itself that confers permission to engage in otherwise proscribed conduct.*

**Ancient definition**
The word License came from the Latin Licentious which means lacking restraint ignoring whatever society standards are imposed upon a person. The black law

dictionary states that the word "License" is to do an act which would otherwise be deemed unlawful. So by that definition a marriage licence issued by the authorities grants you an unlawful act for which you do not need the gentile paper in the first place.

Biblically you are allowed to take a woman a wife without any gentile state laws. She can be your wife upon an oath that is all which is needed between You, Your spouse and Elohim which seals this oath. An elder needs be present only as a witness if required.

The Most High YHWH never required you to go to State to ask for marriage permission. The marriage is a binding contract between you, your wife and Elohim only. In normal biblical marriage an elder or Rabbi can officiate in order to act as witness to the arrangement for inheritance rights. Normally a Rabbi is not needed if you don't have concern for your inheritance rights, he is simply there for testimony if necessary.

The American saying on the dollar "in God we trust" is simply a lie fostered on the people. If they trusted the Most High they would be telling the people to obey the Torah, the statutes, the judgments and the commandments. Are they doing this in the American or other Euro governments? This is why you are mostly trapped in lies of men. YHWH told us to avoid gentile contracts and do not means not to bind ourself.

The best thing you can do for your marriage is to undo your contract and do a Torah one instead. Get a state divorce, then do a ketubah this is better for you and your children.

**The word fornication developed by the gentiles**

**[7]Fornication**

*Sexual intercourse between a man and a woman who are not married to each other.*

---

[7] http://legal-dictionary.thefreedictionary.com

Under the Common Law, the crime of fornication consisted of unlawful sexual intercourse between an unmarried woman and a man, regardless of his marital status. If the woman was married, the crime was Adultery.

Today, statutes in a number of states declare that fornication is an offense, but such statutes are rarely enforced. On the theory that fornication is a victimless crime, many states do not prosecute persons accused of the offense.

Under modern-day legislation, if one of the two persons who engage in sexual intercourse is married to another person, he (or she) is guilty of adultery. Statutes in some states declare that if the woman is married, the sexual act constitutes adultery on the part of both persons, regardless of the man's marital status.

Fornication is an element of a number of Sex Offenses such as rape, Incest, and seduction.

*Word History:* The word *fornication* had a lowly beginning suitable to what has long been the low moral status of the act to which it refers. The Latin word *fornix,* from which *fornicātiō,* the ancestor of *fornication,* is derived, meant "a vault, an arch." The term also referred to a vaulted cellar or similar place where prostitutes plied their trade. This sense of *fornix* in Late Latin yielded the verb *fornicārī,* "to commit fornication," from which is derived *fornicātiō*, "whoredom, fornication." Our word is first recorded in Middle English about 1303.

The American Heritage® Dictionary of the English Language, Fourth Edition copyright ©2000 by Houghton Mifflin Company. Updated in 2009. Published by Houghton Mifflin Company. All rights reserved.

**The Torah**
It has no such word identifications and only identities Adultery as something that can occur if a woman is married. The man may be married or unmarried his status is not necessary. In other words a man married

or unmarried who has sexual relations with a married woman makes them both adulterers. However a married man who has sexual relations with a single woman does not make him an adulterer nor a fornicator as the term is a misappropriation of the word as outlines above for a prostitute a late development in the English language.

**Closing remarks on marriage and divorce**

Some Rabbis say that my view is a hyper-view and that we can divorce as per the Jewish traditions and how Talmud has suggested. I agree that there are many prevailing Jewish scholars and their views including those penned in the Talmud. There are many schools of thought. Know this we are not Ashkenazi Jews who converted to our faith but we are Y'sra'elites. I do agree with many rulings of the Talmud which I feel are just and in line with the Torah but I would disagree that one can divorce for burning someone's food and yes that did too happen. Our original Talmud which was plainly oral was corrupted by adding many new laws to it by Khazarian and Edomite converts so we cannot call these entire laws safe any longer hence why we have to sift though the correct rules of law.

However I wish and desire to follow as YHWH has directed. I know that this is the hardest way to live. There are also questions about what if your wife says I want a divorce and I do not care about what you think. A husband could say the same thing to a wife. They could say we live in such and such government laws which allows it.

My only prayer and hope is that I will submit to Master Yahushua and not make the mistakes made by my predecessors. I submit to His Torah/law and His council. If husbands or wives wish to take the matter into their own hands and divorce the other party then no one can stop that but one day they will have to stand before God and give account of this. They may choose to be oblivious now and commit what our Master termed adultery in Matthew 19:9 by divorcing their spouse and then go marry another, (note only in the case of a woman and not man) so if that happens we just have to leave it in His hands. Such women will not be increased neither in this world or the world to come!!! So for women before you commit your marriage please make sure that your decision is grounded on to stick for life and not six months or six years!!!

# Chapter 3

## *Ancient pattern of North and South placement*

Our forefathers placed wives in the North and South of the country of sojourn.

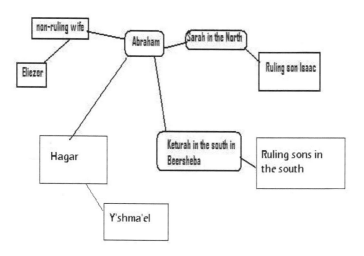

Abraham had four wives listed as follows:

1 Keturah
2 Sarah
3 Mashek
4 Hagar

Sara was the name of an African tribe so Sarah was titled Sar-ee, Abraham's wife was his half sister Gen 20:12, her real name is not given but she was given the title Sara which later was changed by YHWH to Sara-h by appending the heh character to it she became Sar-ah. It was common custom and is still common custom that is strictly followed in the Muslims today to marry patrilineal nieces or cousins. My younger brother who is still a Muslim is married to his patrilineal niece and of course my niece too. There is nothing wrong with it and it is perfectly acceptable according to the Torah to wed your patrilineal niece or cousins.

In ancient Hebrew the name Sarah does not mean a "princess", this is only in rabbinic modernism and Christendom's boot licking of the Zionist Jews who are not the chosen to misapplying modern tenants of the Hebrew language. Today's written or spoken Hebrew is nothing like ancient Hebrew and ancient Hebrew has not been revived yet. We are perhaps at the beginning phases of revival of the language which is far from over. When God restores real Y'sra'el back, many Black Negroes will be seen in Y'sra'el who are the true chosen stock while today's Y'sra'el is simply many gentiles calling themselves Jews. The only true people in Y'sra'el who could be classified chosen are the Black Hebrews in Dimona and Falashas the sons of Melek Solomon from the House of Dawud.

In Ancient Hebrew script the letters sin, resh and yud meant "A bright distinguished bird" which is the term Sari. Note in the ancient Egyptian culture it was very common to see birds, cats, dogs, and other such animals as symbols which clearly reveals ancient Y'sra'el's stock and colour of black. The same is actually true in ancient Hebrew but since it was lost to the real Black Hebrew people more research needs to be done in this area. Also in ancient Iraq (Babylon) the lion was a common symbol. Each culture had its special ancient symbols.

Abraham's wife Sarah was a fair beautiful black woman hence the term and title of Sari was to reveal she was a princess of the tribe of Chad. She was the ruling matriarch in her tribe as many African women were and their sons became the matrilineal Kings. Many questions arise from the text in Genesis. If Abraham was already married to Ketu-rah and had children at fifty then why does Abraham say "I remain childless" (Gen 15:2)? How is it that the scholars have never addressed this issue?

This is because the text in the King James and most other Bibles is simply a bad translation of the Hebrew.

> **Beresheeth (Gen) 15:2** But Abram said, Adoni YHWH, what will You give me, seeing I go

without heir, and he, the son of Mashek[8] Eli'ezer of Damascus is over my Beyth (house)?

The difference is night and day.

Adoni (my master), followed by YHWH. The word is not Adonai; but Adoni YHWH, in English that would be, Master or Lord. Remember Hebrew has gone through at least four stages of development. Today's modern Hebrew Script is not written the same way as did the ancient script which was written in hieroglyphs like the ancient Egyptian language with pictures. Many word meanings were extended and even different from the modern Hebrew.

For some strange reason the verse in Genesis 15:2 which reads in plain Hebrew "The son of Mashek of my house" while it was obscured in its intended meaning has been corrected in this edition. The Hebrew letters are "ובן־משק ביתי."

Abraham's third wife who was likely Keturah's maid she would have come from bilateral trade agreements between Abraham's father Terach another black man who managed a large part of the Euphrates river under the rulership of Nimrod the Black Cushite King in South-Eastern Turkey where Abraham was born. Mashek would have been the maid of Ketu-rah as was Hagar the princess the maid of Sarah. Ketu-rah was the daughter of Joktan who would have had a hand in giving Mashek to Ketu-rah. Abraham had four wives two of which came from the hand maids of his earlier wives. As can be seen Abraham placed his wives North and South. He placed Sarah in the North the princess ruling wife and he placed Princess Hagar in the South. Her son Y'shma'el had a rule in the Egyptian dynasties and we know all of the ancient Egyptian dynasties were Black.

Abraham was a man of black colour of Negro Origin an Abrahu (Hebrew). Mashek was a Turkic woman the daughter of Japheth or what you may term Caucasian. These people were later partly conquered by the Hittites

---

[8] Abraham's third wife who was likely Keturah's maid.

in Turkey. They had land holdings in ancient Y'sra'el such as Hebron where Abraham purchased a field from Ephron.(Gen 23:6-18) and he was recognized as a prince amongst the Hittite people which would have this confirmation from Turkey that Abraham was of Noble Birth.

It is uncommon for women to be referenced as mothers unless there is a special case in point. Abraham took Mashek as wife while he was still in South-Eastern Turkey. Since she was not a ruling princess the text is silent about her. The English translators both modern Ashkenazim Jews and English could not see below the text what is going on and took deliberately to omit the real meaning of the text. This is why it is easy to see why much of the Biblical text is mistranslated and hidden away the true Y'sra'elites under the layers. If you purchase the Hidden-Truth Hebraic Scrolls they will help you study these things out and they can be acquired from www.african-israel.com.

The real Hebrew language was a monosyllable language just like the Egyptian script and did not originally have two or three letter roots in its makeup while this is simply the development of Hebrew from the ancient cultures. The second letter or the third letter only gave more meaning to the first letter so whenever you decipher an ancient Hebrew word always look at the first character. The meaning is embedded in that. Here is a prime example.

The Letter Yod or Yud 👁 it is the picture of an eye. So what would be the meaning of this ancient character on its own?

The idea of the all Seeing Eye is not new but very ancient. The meaning would be simply the opposite of not seeing. So if we can see what do we have? We have the following:

**LIGHT, VISION AND BRIGHTNESS**

If we cannot see then we have darkness, un-illumined, no vision. These are binary opposites. The ancient Hebrews were of a binary culture. Light/dark, sun/moon, earth/sky, man/woman, and hot/cold etc.

Hence the meaning of the Yud is "LIGHT." Did Yahushua declare anything of this? Yes, he did. So those of you who have a hard time with how can he be God, it is embedded in the Yud and He declared it. He operated in the same binary culture that I speak about while the culture you are seeing today in the majority of the world except in Islamic, African and Asian lands is binary too. The same rules apply to African tribes still living today in the African continent.

> **Yahuchannan 8:12** Then spoke Yahushua again to them, saying, <u>I am the **LIGHT** of the world</u>: he that follows me shall not walk in darkness, but shall have the light[9] of life.

In fact the above truth is hidden from many and this is the reason why the Jehovah's witnesses peddle their fake white "Jesus" who is only the Son of Elohim and an angel. The Muslims peddle the created man Esa at least he is middle-eastern/African, which by definition is of the right colour but wrong substance, the Christian Christ who is also allegedly white and a rosy looking Slav Blonde with blue eyes actually the image of the illegitimate son of Pope Alexander called Borgia Cesare, look at the House of Borgia link below. Essentially the Caucasian Jesus is a falsehood perpetuated unto the people, while the real Yahushua was of Black skin colour; please see my book Yahushua – The Black Messiah.

http://en.wikipedia.org/wiki/House_of_Borgia

Are you seeing Borgia Cesare in your visions?

The Christian version at least has the correct heavenly attributes but wrong everything else and also in the Christian perverted trinity we have three He's. Unless I am mistaken and you can tell I am not how can a man produce offspring from another man? The Holy Spirit the Ruach Ha Kadosh is feminine the Mother and not a He. See Article below:

---

[9] Light meaning He is the living Torah. See Ps 119:105, Ps 118:27 and Pro 6:23. He who does not walk in the living which is written Torah does not have life in Messiah because He lives lawlessly.

http://www.african-
Y'sra'el.com/Simon/pdfs/Is%20the%20Holy%20Spirit%
20masculine%20or%20feminine.pdf

It is clear to me and many of us, who hold any understanding of the ancient Hebrew and the culture that Sarah our matriarch who was Lot's sister and Lot is an Egyptian name, note Nim-lot an Egyptian name and Nim-rod are similar. Nim-lot was an ancient High Priest in Thebes likely a descendant of Lot. Thebes is not the original name of the Egyptian city and is a later derivative also.

> **Encyclopedia Britannica**
> The ancient name of Thebes was Wase, or Wo'se. The nome (province) of Wase, the fourth of Upper Egypt, is known to have existed from the 4th dynasty onward. The earliest monuments that have survived at Thebes proper date from the 11th dynasty (2081–1939 bce), when the local nomarchs (governors) united Egypt under their rule. From this time Thebes frequently served as the royal capital of Egypt and was called Nowe, or Nuwe ("City of Amon"), named for its chief god. The Greek name Thebes (Thebai) may have been derived from Ta-ope, the ancient Egyptian name for ... (100 of 3150 words)

Nim-rod or Nim-rut the son of Cush (Ethiopian/Sudanese, Nubian Empires) was related to Abraham's family. These were black African people who traveled from West Africa to the Northern Turkic Hemisphere by conquering nations. This is how both Abraham's father Terach and Nimrod ended up working for each other, clans followed each other.

Nimrod's brother Rammah was ruling in West Africa which included rule in Eastern Arabia today known as Saudi Arabia. This is how the early Arabs ended up being Black Africans. Africa had an amazing great culture nothing seen in our modern times, they far surpassed it. The reason why the Caucasians quickly erased black history was due to two reasons one the curses of the Torah for Torah violations that fell on the ancient Y'sra'elite black people and two the hatred seen among the white people of today for people of colour whether they be Mexican, Latin, American or some other nationals for what we call Black racism. Yes it does exist in all parts of the corporate and non corporate Caucasian world. This is not to say it does not exist amongst the blacks but it is a lot more severe in these Caucasian races. When people like Napoleon's soldiers saw the Sphinx of a black man they could not resist but to shoot it down in disgust. How could a black man be painted so great must have be their reasoning for shooting its nose off?

Notice the Caucasians did this to many Egyptian sculptures breaking the noses is another evidence that the sons of Japheth acted their fullest into deceiving others since a long time. Yapet mean 'High Head' in ancient Hebrew and a man of two tongues. The only time the sons of Japheth can be trusted is when they have joined Y'sra'el and renounced all their worldly idolatries. Yapet will act out his nature so beware. Just look at their history how they ruled nations by deception.

The Egyptian pyramids were made to look like made by Indian looking Egyptians by European handlers, while this is not an accurate picture of ancient Pharaohs who were of African Black stock.

The bright and best men of Y'sra'el were made to look like white, have you ever wondered why to propagate the superiority of the white race which is another myth? Abraham, Isaac, Ishmael, Musa, Joshua, King Dawud and King Solomon were great black men. King Solomon a man of colour surpassed all the wisdom of Egypt and all other nations put together. This reality has irked so many people that he is no longer painted in his original colour Black but as a white Caucasian.

Just look at ancient Egypt pictures presented to the modern world in TV. Nimrod built a tower that I have not seen even built in modern times to the same height and breadth so think about it before you run down ancient cultures. Granted that he built a tower in defiance to God but the modern towers in America were nothing in comparison to what he built and if you think the rich Americans are building towers to glorify God sorry this is not true. The Arabs may not have the true God but when they build towers they have their deity Allah in mind while Europe and America have become countries where atheism seems to be prospering and the God of Abraham is left in the backseat so to speak. Christians in that nation bemoan the removal of the Ten Commandments from schools and governmental places but they never follow the Torah.

Even the ubiquitous dollar bill has the symbol of the free masons "All seeing eye" on the pyramid on the back of the dollar bill which actually is the original symbol of YHWH so what is the point of putting "in God we trust" upon the note if at the same time you entertain free masonry and occultism? Have we not realized yet that we are destined to fall if we mix worship with idolatry? Then which God one should worship Mammon or YHWH?

Even the ego today represents similar to Nimrod to say that I can defy you the Creator and build great structures. I know it may be hard to admit our mistakes but realties are very different when viewed from cold facts on the ground. We must look at our self and do some soul searching to see if what we are doing is magnifying God or seeking to exalt our self as great men and women. Even the Brazilian people who built the image of the western Jesus had the Creator in mind but at least they wanted to represent who they worshipped. In fact this is proof that people of color think very differently. They always have behind their minds how to honor their Creator. So these people would only do what they know best and one cannot blame them for erecting images when they know no better. In ancient Egypt people built big images to their deities and to their heroes. Today the Caucasian culture follows that pattern without admitting where they got this pattern.

Ancient Egyptian people were black Africans with the same kind of hair that eventually was also found with the Master Yahushua as African locks. Surprised, but you should not be if you were really seeking after the truth. I would not expect to see any different, a man of wooly hair which even if left undone becomes locked. No, he was not Caucasian and he certainly did not come out of the Zagreb Mountains looking like a Caucasian son of Yapet. I expect an African man to look like an African no matter which region he lives in he must carry African traits. One of the things he spoke about is His Father's house. This is an African term in the ancient culture where the chief's house is in the middle with all the other elders around the main house. The Temple was also built in similar style in the middle of Y'sra'el where all the other houses of the Hebrews were around about the Temple.

One of the key questions I ask people who claim to have seen our Master is what colour was He, please describe His skin colour and hair type, what type and description of his body features? It may seem like silly questions but it is meant to weed out the chaff. To date I have not found a single person who has described his facial makeup or hair type correctly which is why I can reject the western white "Jesus" that many keep seeing in their dreams and visions due to too much TV and Roman Catholicism unfortunately has corrupted people's minds and false visions.

These types of people become very upset at the white 'Jesus' they have seen or perhaps describe. If they are challenged that He is not white then they will look for the nearest exit to leave and make their excuses and go.

I have only found one woman who described Satan to me with absolute clarity and correctly, she is British and saw him on the edge of She'ol/Hell and was indeed correct in her description of him as of Black colour. Angels are also black. Satan is Jet black also with a princely forehead and he can change himself in various ways. She saw him become like a bulldog and that scared the living daylights out of her but she knew what she had seen was the real deal. She also saw the

Master but could not describe him as was not privy to His face or body because she just saw light surrounding a person from a distance on the edge of She'ol (paradise). Her description was accurate of her vision/dream which indicated to me that she was telling the truth.

The Master may increase her for her true testimony. Another British woman a famous Muslim convert on the other hand who has claimed that she saw the twelve disciples descended in her room is a false embellished testimony and totally unreliable so we need to be careful not to run off after visions which may not be what we think they are. Some visions are reliable and must come to pass while others are not.

He showed me a glimpse of how it feels to lose someone you love so much and that is the pain our Father in heavens feels for Y'sra'el who he will restore.

**Keturah**

Abraham's wife Keturah lived in the South and was likely his first wife followed by Sarah as his second wife and then the third wife Mashek followed by the fourth Hagar who was the daughter of the Pharaoh of Egypt which was given to Abraham as a gift when he came out of Egypt (Genesis 12:20). That is when Abraham had made an agreement with Pharaoh. The text clearly tells you she was an Egyptian in Genesis 16:1, which tells us where she came from and she was not just an ordinary woman but the daughter of Pharaoh an important princess while most of you have just made her a mistress of Abraham and almost de-legitimized her. All the ancient Pharaoh's were black and so was she which means Y'shma'el was Black in complexion too. Ancient Y'sra'el was an African country now read between the lines.

The text of Yashar 12:59 (The book of Jasher) tells us that Eli'ezer was a gift to Abraham but if you thought that he came wrapped in a package with a ribbon attached to it then this will be a mistake. It was Eli'ezer's mother Mashek that was a gift to Abraham as a wife in the Northern Alliance but she then gave birth to Eli'ezer as Abraham's concubine/wife. Mashek was from Damascus which explains that Nimrod ruled this area in order to give a woman here as a gift to Abraham. (Note I told you earlier they were related)

According to Yashar 13:5 Abraham was fifty years old when YHWH came to him to ask him to leave the land with his wives and household. This indicates to us that at fifty Abraham was already married but notice that in Yashar 12:59 Eli'ezer is a grown up young man which proves that Abraham was already married to Keturah from which the gift of the maid his third wife came to him because she was connected to Keturah's family side and Keturah was already living in Canaan/Y'sra'el so Abraham was familiar with the land of Y'sra'el as a child because his father often went to visit the land to meet his wife (Abraham's mother) there and Abraham would have visited the land as a baby also.

When I first came to faith I was told the bad teachings that Abraham never visited the land but later on examining scriptures by the Spirit of YHWH (The mother Ruach Ha Kadosh) prompted me to re-look in Genesis to see and understand that Abraham was very familiar with the land he was sent to. Ancient Y'sra'el was a nation with lots of little kingdoms. It was not a single nation like the USA today or the UK with one central government. If you look at 15$^{th}$ century Africa then Y'sra'el was like that. In the African continent there were over hundred kingdoms with local chiefs, princess and kings. This was like Y'sra'el. We read about it in Joshua 5:1, 2:1, 7:2. Yericho was one kingdom and Ai another. Y'sra'el being an Afro centric nation had the same model.

Abraham was from the priestly Horoite clan and it is historically known that the Horoites lived in Bethlehem in ancient times. The Horoites believed in Horus as the son of god and that he will one day come down as the son of god as a man and wear the two crowns.

Abraham's mothers was in Beersheba who would have controlled water wells and his father controlled the water resources in the North of the river Euphrates and its tributaries as the king's (Nimrod) General and High

Priest in his army. He maintained Nimrod's temple of idols/figurines of their ancestors and Abraham was the next in line had he followed his father's false religion (Josh 24:14). This also indicates Terach had two wives one in the south who was Abraham's mother and one in the north who was Abraham's step mum. Nimrod was one of the first few gebborim (Mighty warrior and Tyrant) so to speak. He was Cushite Black from Northern Sudan where you find tall people since he was also tall and very strong.

Who was Abraham's first born son Isaac or Ishmael? Actually neither, Yoktan (Yokshan) is the firstborn of Keturah she lived in Beersheba and Abraham was already married to Keturah before he acquired Hagar as his fourth wife, she was an Egyptian princess (Gen 16:1) so therefore Y'shma'el's birth is not the first birth though Y'shma'el is the firstborn son of princess Hagar.

Keturah likely to be the first wife named her son in her great grandfather Joktan's (Gen 10:25) name which was the common custom and is shown with others too in the Torah such as Ytzhak and Yaqub. Abraham had two wives followed by Mashek the third wife given to him by Keturah through Nimrod and Sarah giving him Hagar an Egyptian princess which totals four wives. Sarai is not the name of a woman but a black tribe and one that exits in Africa so this reveals Abraham's black ancestors. Sarai (my princess), the modern Jews believe that Y'skah was Abraham's wife Sarah however this is not true as Sarah was from Tarach's second wife Abraham's half sister as he stated in Gen 20:12. In ancient Hebrew Y'skah means "Beautiful bright creature."

The ancient Yud was the picture of an eye 👁 hence why the term bright. Sarah was a beautiful light brown skinned woman. If I compared her to a modern black woman then Halle Berry would be it though I would go further and say Sarah was even prettier than Halle Berry in her description.

Though the moon does not have any of its own light but reflects the sun's light so this is not a description of her colour as of the moon but just her beauty since the

ancient Samech is the picture of the moon. ☽.
Remember I spoke earlier about ancient Hebrew language looked like Egyptian language and was originally a monosyllable language. The first character is what mattered but the additional characters gave meaning or shape to the first character. In order to know meaning of the character the first character is what did it. Now that sets up all the scholarship on its head that claims that Hebrew is made of two letter roots. Not true.

Sarah was Abraham's half sister (Sister Wife) and Keturah was his cousin wife from Mother's side Matrilineal. We find the pattern in the Tanach of people of noble birth or princes having at least two wives one from the father's side and one from the mother's side. This was common practice in African/Asian cultures and is even today. Note all three women Sarah, Hagar and Keturah were black women and the ancestors of the African people while the Gnostic literature written much after the gospels between 70 and 400 CE depicts them as white which is falsified text and should not be relied upon for Abraham's family line. Keturah would have been taking care of the family inheritance home of Abraham in the south while Sarah would have been taking care of the inheritance home in the north in Shechem. Keturah's six sons eventually ruled the whole of the Arabian Peninsula. The Rabbis incorrectly teach people that Keturah and Hagar are the same once again deliberately causing confusion. Note these rabbis are not the chosen people see my book Yahushua the Black Messiah in which I detail who are the chosen and why these European converts cannot call them the chosen.

This is a false Zionist teaching beware that they are the chosen as they are not. They spoon feed these kinds of erroneous teachings to church seminaries who then spew out this type of error under the auspices of the Zionist rabbis.

Abraham was a prince and chief (Gen 23:6). Such type of people always had at least two wives with lineages from both parents while they often also took extra wives to protect the property and extend the sons to regions under their control. Hagar was of Egyptian descent which was part of the North African region so she would have controlled territory in the south in the Egyptian/Arabia region.

# Chapter 4
## *Polygany or Monogamy what was Y'sra'el's true lifestyle?*

Y'srae'lite men did not know what monogamy is as the majority of black Y'sra'elite men had plural wives. If you want to see go and look in Jamaica today the ones who were freed slaves are real Y'sra'elites. Even after colonialism they still do not accept the British customs of a single wife and they have always gone for more than one wife. Jamaicans are from the tribe of Asher and Yisschar the word Jamaican is an evolved word and not what they really are.

Many of the people who espouse monogamy based on a faulty outlook usually and always cite two passages. We will look at this in detail today.

They usually cite the passage in Genesis 2:22

> **Genesis 2:22** (KJV) And the rib, which the LORD God had taken from man, made he a woman, and brought her unto the man.

The Christians who usually cite this are the worst in the bunch of people who have the audacity to cite passages from the Torah when they are just Paulitions and into Pauline Christianity where the Torah of YHWH has been abrogated for them according to the deceitful Paul and their Torahless Church fathers. They should be ashamed that when they need to talk about marriage they either use the passages from our Torah which speaks about polygamy and not monogamy and their apostle of deceit Paul who they use to abrogate the laws who to this day many of them do not even know was not commissioned by God. Now let me show you how many women YHWH actually created.

First woman/wife of Adam

**Gen 1:27** So Elohim created ha'Ahdahm in His own images, in the images of Elohim He created him; male and female He created them.

The first woman that was created with Ahdahm was Lilith for his wife. Note both were created from the ground, Lilith was animated by the vapor see note Gen 2:6, while Chava his second wife (Patriarchal wife) was created from Ahdahm's side. The first woman became rebellious to her husband and ran away by using the set-apart name of Elohim, which then brought the need to create the second woman for Ahdahm.

Second woman/wife of Adam

> **Gen 2:22** And the side with the bone, which YHWH Elohim had taken from man, he made woman, and brought to the man.

Third woman/wife of Adam

> **Gen 2:23** And Ahdahm said, at this reoccurrence, These standing in front of my face are bones of my bones, and flesh of my flesh: they shall be called Ishah (woman), because these were taken out of her Husband.

Ha'Paam in the ancient Hebrew hieroglyph has the character of the Heh, the Head for Peh, the Ayin to walk and Mem for plural waters, it means women standing in front of him. The Heh is not just the term 'The' but "THESE" meaning more than one.

The Hebrew word צלעת (Zalot) here is plural, bones, and not, a single bone. Those who argue, for a single rib, can not address the Hebrew language showing us, plural bones, which indicates the creation of two women at the same time.

The same Hebrew word can also denote a wife or wives, so Adam could have been calling her his wife and not just a woman, these were two women created here one which was placed in the North axis and the other which was placed in the south axis, see Genesis

12 and Genesis 25 for an explanation of the North and South meanings.

To protect from incest a brother and sister cannot marry so Qayin who is mentioned in Genesis 4 could not have married Adam and Eve (Chava's) daughter which would be incest. God would not send them out of the Garden for sin to go and correct their sin and then allow them to continue in sin. This is the type of false teachings in the churches.

A brother and a sister who are from the same mother and father cannot marry, which is a sin but a brother and a sister from different wives of the same husband are allowed to marry as was Abraham and his wife from Terach's second wife see Gen 11:29 and Gen 20:12.

Therefore the question can be easily answered that Qayin's wife came from Adam's third wife that was his half sister but not biological sister as this kind of marriage was forbidden as incest was never permitted at any time (Lev 18:9). God is the not the author of neither sin nor confusion. This role is being played out by the church becoming the author's of confusion and sin while confusion brings chaos and mayhem into peoples lives and a false sense of peace. While this fact that Adam had plural marriages in the Garden is not something evident to the people who read the bibles with the faulty translations. They attribute to God sin by saying God allowed incest in the beginning. Where does it say God ever allowed sin? This is how sinful minds think.

Ruler priests always had two wives at minimum where one wife was placed in the South and one in the North, we see this with both Abraham and his father. Terach's one wife was living in Bethlehem and the other in Turkey the pattern of the North and South. Abraham had his wife Keturah in the south and his wife Sarah in the North. We find this pattern time and time again indicating that ruler/priests such as Abraham always kept two households. Apparently most modernist don't know two are better than one.

One might wonder how such a thing or arrangement can work. It even works today either you have both of your wives in one city each or even in two separate countries as did Abraham's father Terach. If you are living in the West and you had to support a wife in the east it would be much easier without any complications provided the woman is sincere where you could visit her two to three times a year and spend time with her. You could potentially go over there in that nation or she could also come to visit you in the country of your sojourn. This arrangement would be such eventually allowing you to make a choice for living together with all your wives.

If you kept your wife in two cities as Abraham did then it's not a problem there either as you could easily travel between cities to manage your wives in. Some may wish to keep them in the same home however this may work for some but it does not complete the formation of the North/South divide in which there is a great spiritual increase. It's not about how many wives you can squeeze into one house because women do not like to share things with other sister wives. Some women are more jealous than others and this can play out in the home and cause great amount of problems. When you keep them separate then you also allow fewer problems to be created. One may argue against this but the reality is that this pattern has shown to work for our forefathers so this method is unquestionable.

Our people never practiced western style monogamy as that was adopted by the west from the Roman rule. Greeks also had the same kind of model. In the Roman rule it was one wife and one boyfriend (mixed sexual relations forbidden to us) or one wife and one mistress and if you look around in the western lands you can see the model has not changed. In reality these people live in very unrighteous lifestyles but not according to the laws of the Torah but according to personal choices. However since we are Y'sra'elites we are commanded not to follow the customs of the nations yet many Y'sra'elites have adopted the corrupt western Christendom lifestyles.

**Deut 13:6** Suppose your own full brother, or

your son, or your daughter, or your beloved wife, or your friend, which are very close to you, entertain you by secretively, saying, Let us go and **serve other powers**, which You have not known, You, nor your ahvot (fathers); **7** Namely, of the powers of the people which are roundabout you, near to you, or far off from you, from the one end of the country even to the other end of the world;

Aren't many of you saying we should be subservient to other powers or we should subject to the government? Yes some of them are saying that and using the likes of the corrupt deceitful self proclaimed apostle Paul of the New Testament to do just that. They read Romans 13 to teach people we must be subject. They use Paul to force people not only to abandon the laws of YHWH which is forbidden but you make them subject to the humiliation of the gentiles. This apostle of deceit has been dealt with by us and we have a number of teachings on him on our website at www.african-israel.com. We are not going to be entrapped by such people because when we apply the parameters of Deuteronomy 13 we find him a false apostle and prophet. None of his prophecies ever came to pass but I doubt you have examined him at any length. He also denied the deity of Messiah by calling him First Born over all creation.

>**Col 1:15** Who is the image of the invisible Elohim, the firstborn of all creation:

Paul used an idolatrous pagan concept to define the Messiah as an image which is the Greek word Ikon. Well if the Messiah is an image (Ikon) then that is idolatry defined by Paul leading people into more idolatry. Then he said the Messiah is the firstborn meaning he is created as a man. This further reveals Paul's corrupt theology. In Phil 2:7 he used a pagan concept of God emptying himself as a man as if to remove from himself one attribute at a time, this cannot be possible as is a pagan concept and is well known by Roman Catholic high clergy that the statement is irrelevant and not true, it cannot be applied to the God of Y'sra'el. They teach their people to ignore that statement as it's from pagan sources. Only pagan gods removed their attributes and became men so to speak.

The Messiah is YHWH revealed in the flesh because that is what John 1:1 spoke about refuting Pauline false theologies.

No matter how good it feels we are forbidden to neither follow after the heathen customs nor follow their gods. The powers in the passage of Deut 13:6 refer not only to their gods but also to their leadership who make sinful rules so that the people break the Torah and its laws. One such rule in these nations is that you can have same gender marriages which are forbidden in the Torah. The other rule they follow is that you can follow after their custom of marriage in Churches. This too is forbidden to us as they invoke the names of false deities such as the Caucasian 'Jesus' who they have created from the Greco/Roman model and misapplied, the real Master Yahushua is not white and not Torahless which according to their false priesthood is. If you have taken the name of the false man-made name of Jesus then that law or vow cannot bind you. The only oath that binds us is in the name of YHWH and not some English concoction called 'Jesus'.

The Messiah had a real name and it was not Jesus an appellation made up five hundred years ago by the gentile world. His real name was Yahushua in the Hebrew text. Now we will also look at the objection the gentiles raise up for polygyny by using the deceitful apostle Paul and his letters which have no eternal value.

> 1Ti 3:12 (KJV) Let the deacons be the husbands of one wife, ruling their children and their own houses well.
>
> Tit 1:6 (KJV) If any be blameless, the husband of one wife, having faithful children not accused of riot or unruly.

Now pagan churchmen are going to teach the real Hebrews how to live not using Torah but using the corrupt deceitful apostle Paul who was rejected by the first century disciples and they never called him an apostle though he keeps calling himself one.

First of all Paul does not have the position to issue halacha but only to state what is already agreed in the Torah. The Torah permits more than one wife so therefore by definition whoever translated the above passage this being the scholars of King James Version text who were forty-seven gentiles they would be wrong to say one wife in both of the above passages since Y'sra'el as a society in ancient times was polygamous. Y'sra'el is also an African country and not a European one so African people have always had polygamy and even this is true today while those who try to impose their European centric model of slavery such as the scholars of King James failed to interpret the passages correctly. We reject all such Greco-Roman interpretations. Torah comes first then the prophets and Paulos in the schemes of things is last and his letters are just letters. His letters are history and that is only how they will be treated. He is not an apostle and will be given no such rank.

Ruling chiefs always placed two wives in the North/South divide see extensive research done by Alice C. Linsley at Just Genesis for thirty-three years on this at http://jandyongenesis.blogspot.com. Our people were black Y'sra'elites and polygamy is very common to our people in Africa and still is.

Here is how the passage should have been translated as in the HTHS (Hidden-Truths Hebraic Scrolls).

> **First Timotheous 3:12** Let the attendants be the husbands of at least one wife, ruling their children and their own batyim (houses) well.
>
> **Titus 1:6** If any be blameless, the husband of at least one wife, having faithful children not accused of rebellion or unruly.

Since Torah allows polygamy and if a leader such as Moses can have two wives there is no reason that an overseer or Bishop cannot be married to two women and living a Torah centered life. The passage was deliberately mistranslated due to Roman, Greek influence of the translators. The word Akhad does not always mean just one because two people such as a husband and a wife are called Akhad (United One), the plurality of YHWH is called Akhad (One). Day and night are called akhad (one) yet are seen as two elements of a 24 hour period. The Aramaic term Khad is the same as the Hebrew term Akhad, however no matter what one argues all the scriptures were written in Hebrew first, not Greek and not Aramaic. So as a Rabbi must be married therefore in order to be a Rabbi a teacher of the law must have at least one wife.

> Messianic Rabbi Joe Vial a Hebrew scholar adds:
>
> 1 Tim. 3:2 The Aramaic reads: b'khada antatah (by one wife), in other words he must have at least one wife, or else as a single man he would be open to the vilest temptations. The anti-polygamy campaigners take note that if you think Rabbi Paulos bans polygamy then we have nothing to do with Rabbi Paulos and his letters because then you all have to ban Rabbi Paulos by your own definition of being in ministry because he did not have one wife yet Rabbi Paulos was married in order to be a Rabbi. Torah allows polygyny and that is how it stands!

So it's clear that in Torah it is allowed to have more than one wife and each man and woman has to weigh up this need for them. Now let us look at the argument that Romans 13 tells us not to break the laws of the land.

> **Romans 13**:1 (KJV) Let every soul be subject unto the higher powers. For there is no power but of God: the powers that be are ordained of God.

So I am told by the religious elite or scholarly Christians that YHWH appointed Nero to skin Christians alive! This is the incredible fiction that we are led to believe and for this so many peoples lives stand ruined. I am sorry to say that this is not how the laws of God see things even if those in clergy haven't a clue what they are talking about, it can never stand. They need to throw away their diplomas and degrees and just go and learn from the orthodox Rabbis in Y'sra'el what and how to interpret scripture and if they don't then they will just continue to put other people in misery and error.

So when the bible tells us that we are to stand against evildoers this would mean I would have to give in to the likes of Hitler, Pol Pot and Saddam while they murdered innocent civilians. Only unwise gentiles can believe this.

God's appointed leaders do not do what Nero did; secondly the Scripture above or Paul non-canonical letters says something so radically different, that you are going to look silly when you interpret in such a way to apply it to your local government that approves sodomy, gay marriages and of course the ubiquitous assisted suicide known as Euthanasia. Today many governments approve abortion which is nothing short of murdering babies. Well unless I want to be completely stupid and an idiot on top to believe that this is all fine and dandy for the God of Y'sra'el who appointed life for His people and not death, which is unlikely not for me at least and those I stand to correct!

Let us look at the Hidden-Truths Hebraic Scrolls translation:

> **Romans 13:1** Let every man be subordinate to the governing authorities *of the Temple*. For there is no authority but that of Elohim: the governing authorities are established by Elohim.

Here is what it means

Paul has been discussing Y'sra'el in the last three chapters and so here he does the same for non-Jews (Ten tribes and other nations grafting in to Y'sra'el) explaining how they fit into the Hebrew Yahudim worldview. The powers that Paulos speaks of here are not of the local Roman government which is an erroneous view held by Christendom generally, but the powers of the Synagogue that were allied to the power of the Temple. The Temple was in place as the <u>Authority of YHWH</u> and early believers, all went there, and even prayed and celebrated the feasts in the Temple together. They even sacrificed offerings there too. It is hard for people to understand this model today but let's take a look at both examples by looking at the Islamic faith and the Catholic faith.

All mosques align with Mecca in Saudi Arabia and all Catholic churches align with the Vatican in Rome. This is how they celebrate their feasts such as Christmas and Eid. Going by this model this means Saudi Arabia is the place of authority for Muslims while for Catholics the Pope's authority issues out of the Vatican in Italy.

If another person claiming to be the Pope Issues authority out of another country then that would be rejected, the same applies to Islam.

Once we understand this then we can move forward. Therefore, the only authority structure that was ordained by YHWH in Jerusalem was the Temple institute and all the synagogues where early Nazarenes met; these were indeed kosher to go to for worship and praise which did indeed happen with the early believers. The Yahudim are our brothers and remain so; nothing has changed except that there is no Temple system in Jerusalem right now. It is highly suspect for us to believe that the higher authorities ordained by YHWH is Rome or our present governments they are not and people like Nero who slaughtered Christians and skinned them alive!!!

Is Paul saying that you cannot break the law under any circumstances?
Hopefully next time you will know the truth far better than now and you will act with wisdom. I hope that you will not stand for tyranny.

Let us just take a look at one particular law of the land and see what you think.

The Shi'ite law in Iran which still exists in some parts of Iran today is that when a woman is married to a husband, the Imam (cleric) of that town must spend the first night with her and deflower her. Does that seem right and lawful according to the arguments of the people who say you must believe in the law of the land?

If we all had to agree on this law then the wife of the believing husband would be defiled and committing adultery according to the biblical law. This means that she and the Imam would both have to be stoned to death as per the Torah law that is if the Torah was allowed to be enacted in Iran. If we continued in this fashion a newly married man would never obtain a wife and he would ultimately have to resort to asceticism. Or, he would have to leave the land for another nation where he would not have to allow the local cleric to defile his wife.

This is the problem today with some people, who think that it's okay for anyone to break God's Law, which is penned in Torah and that they have to just accept the law of the land as expedient. Does this mean that even a law that goes against God"s word for the believer is just supposed to stand there and pray about it and just accept it? Unfortunately many Christians are hoodwinked to believe this kind of nonsense preached by ignorant pastors.

Accepting this is a sin at best and a heresy at worst. Now in order for our mindset to be qualified to accept this type of law of the land, we would have to prove to ourselves that adultery is allowed in scripture. I know that today in our society adultery is allowed and even encouraged by friends as a kind of excitement to rev up your sexual life at home. Remember, we are talking about the biblical law versus man's laws (futile)! The reality of this is that you will not find it acceptable behavior anywhere in Scripture. We cannot accept sin nor say it is ok because our national laws approve it!!!

Therefore the case for those Christians who want to use this passage in Romans 13:1 to break God's law by banning Torah laws is actually contradictory. But let us look further.

> Romans 13:2 **(KJV) Whosoever therefore resisteth the power, resisteth the ordinance**

**of God: and they that resist shall receive to themselves damnation.**

Is Paul really telling us to uphold governmental laws which go against YHWH? Now let us see a translation with some meat in it.

> **Romiyah 13:2** (HTHS) Whosoever therefore resists the ruling authority, withstands the institution of Elohim, *which is the Temple and synagogues.* They that resist these shall receive judgment to themselves.

It is pretty clear that the ruling authority is the Temple and the Synagogues. We know this is true because even Yahushua did not obstruct them from casting judgment upon Him.

Theoretically, the ordinance of Elohim prevents abuse of law so it is actually a judgment of YHWH and not the local government. They have a good role and overall they did carry out this role.

The judgment/ordinance of YHWH can only be enacted by the standing Temple authority which took place during Paul's time but cannot today as there is no Temple. It is not talking about a local governor or Prime Minister enacting national laws of the land at all. Our Prime Minister just declared same gender marriages are legal in 2012, the president of the USA Barak Obama spoke in favour of same gender marriages also, do you think we are asked to submit to these corrupt heathen authorities? No, not according to YHWH of Y'sra'el. Your governments make many unrighteous rules and laws to promote themselves and fill their coffers once again we have to weigh up everything against the Torah to see if its lawful or unlawful.

Now let me explain a situation that many ex-Muslims like me experienced. They knew and were taught that the first law for them is Islam; and then the laws of the land. Any law of the land that was contradictory to Sha'ria (Islamic law), we were taught to reject it, because we were only to accept the laws of the land that were <u>in line</u> with the Qur'an.

This is my opinion and also the opinion of the highest jurist in Islam, is the correct way to live your Islamic faith for any Muslim. Now how much more that we practice and uphold biblical laws as believers should we uphold the Torah, which is YHWH's law? They come first and not last.

Note we should reject any law of the land that tells us to break any biblical law. How so? If you were a doctor and were told to perform an abortion and that is clear cut murder, then you would have to reject that law even if it means losing your job. I know reality is not that easy and many fall into the trap but look do you want blood on your hands? What If that same child lived and grew up to be a genius? You not only have killed one child by accepting to do the bidding of the state but you would be the murderer of a generation of children because through that one child many other children would have been born. You would be the murderer of a whole clan.

Think about this; is it better to lose your job and save a life, or keep your job and take a life? Are you willing to take a chance that the possible outcome of your performing an abortion is that you could lose your eternal life in Yahushua? Remember if you honor YHWH He will surely honor you and never put you down for it.

Would you as a Rabbi or Pastor go and perform a marriage ceremony for two men which Scripture prohibits and calls it an abomination? Where in scripture will you be searching for your reference if you decide to commit this biblical crime?

Will you look to your local council laws or Paul's letters? Paul's letters are incorrectly interpreted and taken out of context by majority of Christendom today, they practice what I can only term as Pauline Christianity adopted by Roman Catholicism and later by all Anglicans abrogating the Torah. Paul was not an apostle albeit self proclaimed one at that.

That would be very unwise to override established halacha in Torah and revealed in the books of the prophets. Even Paul the Pharisee believed Torah and admitted it in spite of his loose statements and pagan concepts in other letters of his.

Christendom has made a new religion out of Paul's letters and are following the error of Marcionism, who presented the ten cobbled up letters of Paul and made his (Marcion) own NT Document.

### http://en.wikipedia.org/wiki/Marcion_of_Sinope

**Marcion** (Μαρκίων) (ca. 85-160) was an Early Christian theologian who was excommunicated [1] by the Christian church at Rome as a heretic. His teachings were influential during the 2nd century and a few centuries after, rivaling that of the Church of Rome. As he offered an alternative theology to the Canonical, Proto-orthodox, Trinitarian and Christological views of the Roman Church, the early Church Fathers denounced him sharply; their views dominate Christianity today. One of the greatest heretics in church history, he was universally condemned by all branches of the universal Christian church, and even called the first born of Satan.[2]

Marcion is sometimes referred to as one of the gnostics, but from what assessment of his lost writings can be gleaned from his mainstream opponents, his teachings were quite different in nature.[3] His canon included ten Pauline Epistles and one gospel[4] called the Gospel of Marcion, plus a rejection of the whole Hebrew Bible, and did not include the rest of the books later incorporated into the canonical New Testament. He propounded Christianity free from Hebrew teachings with Paul as the reliable source of authentic doctrine. Paul was, according to Marcion, the only apostle who had rightly understood the new message of salvation as delivered by Christ.[5]

Many ex-Muslims have lived under Sha'ria in Great Britain, United States, Canada and other nations, from the day they arrived in these countries. And so did I in my past yet people cry about Sha'ria in Britain today.

I can tell you categorically that we practiced Sha'ria (Islamic law) in our home twenty five years ago. Every Muslim lives it in his home and practices Sha'ria. My relatives living in Britain practice it today! You may ask how? It means they commit marriages by the Islamic law, they commit divorces by the Islamic laws and they recite the Azan (prayer) in a new born child's ear according to Islamic law. I did the same practice for my two children when they were born I had to call an elder from the Mosque to do this.

Now what about amputation of arms and legs of thieves? No problem. This is not done because the laws of the land prevail and Muslims are <u>subjects.</u> However, if they ever come into power, you can bet they will bring these laws here. So what cannot be practiced without proper Islamic jurisprudence, meaning a ruling council is left to the Islamic centers in Saudi Arabia to deal with. This is not to say that Islam is right but to prove my point that even Muslims know that the **FIRST** law of validity is the Islamic law and the rest must either line up or be discarded.

It exists in every Muslim home, do not be deceived!!!

How much more then, should Torah and Biblical laws exist and be obeyed in every home we as believers occupy? Yes it's true we cannot enact some judgments, but we do not have to as they are for the Temple and the Sanhedrin council, which is yet future. We should do our best endeavors, to do everything we can and leave everything we cannot. This is how the prophets lived in the Diaspora and is the correct way to live.

The only authority we submit to is YHWH's and if we are under a human government we know we may not be able to change things but at the same time we are not to accept all the unrighteous laws they make either. Kefa (Peter) said it like this:

**Kefa Alef (First Peter) 2:13-14** Submit

yourselves to the institutions (Rabbinic law courts) for the Master's (Adon's: Lord's) sake: whether it be to the prince/Nasi, as supreme; (14) Or to leaders, as to them that are sent by him for the punishment of evildoers, and for the praise of them that do well.

Which rulers? These are the local rabbinic courts and not unbelieving gentile courts. I am sorry, but the **unbelieving gentiles** just do not cut it in God's ecomony unless they are part of Y'sra'el. In which case they are no longer called **gentiles** but they are Hebrews or Abrahuans.

Note; this is not a human government! This is talking about the institutions such as the Temple in the ancient times. Also other synagogues or other Y'sra'elite type institutions setup by men (Rabbis) whose primary function was to enact YHWH's laws or to teach YHWH's laws such as the School of Hillel. Peter is not talking about the Roman government; they were not executing God's law but their own. Can one twist scripture so much to believe that Titus the Roman ruler who had ripped Yahudi men's stomachs came to enact God's laws? Absolutely not! The whole thrust in Peter's letters is about how the present believers fit into the rabbinic academies that were setup and were trying to exert authority with scripture.

What many of you do not know that Judah is still God's lawgiver!!!!!!

Many Messianic and Christians will always fail, when they cite laws that are against God's laws and they say we must obey them which is absolutely not true. This happens even when they ignorantly stand against Scriptural law such as abortion and homosexuality. Again, if you are a doctor and they tell you to murder a twenty three week old baby in the womb of a woman, would you then cite your human laws of the land while killing the baby and hope this is acceptable to God as well? While YHWH tells you, **Thou shall not murder (Exodus 20:13).** In addition, we are to take action by writing to our Ministers or our Senators but anarchy, hoodlum and breaking windows is not the answer and we do not do that. We need to consider everything prayerfully and only accept what is Scriptural and reject what is not. This is the simple truth. We must not walk in gentile laws where possible the law of our King YHWH is supreme.

This has nothing to do with being governed by civil law, such as being told to believe everything they tell you, while in fact it is the reverse.

Please show me one human **unbelieving gentile** government that did not function to usurp the authority of the people and break the set-apart laws of the bible? Sadly you won't find any. Many also contradict themselves by saying that we are to be in obedience to them, when Scripture is clear that "All **authority** has been given to our Master Yahushua".

> **Matthew 28:18** Then Yahushua came and spoke to them, saying, "**All authority has been given to Me** in heaven and on earth.

How come He has all authority and yet you have to obey some nonsensical laws of a government, which are unscriptural? Christians have been taught many wrong doctrines for far too long. Break the shackles of your church error and live in the freedom that Torah and Messiah offer you. Decide today and walk in freedom or live in the shackles for the rest of your life!!!

Yahushua was not wrong when He said "take my yoke upon you" meaning His Torah, His government and He is also saying "You shall be free indeed". How are you going to be free in the national government laws when clearly many laws of the land break the biblical laws? In Islamic lands the Islamic government will not even let you proclaim the biblical truths in public and in places like Pakistan they will put false charges against you with the blasphemy laws and kill you. Just last week a Christian boy in Pakistan was hacked to death in a police cell on false blasphemy charges. He had done nothing wrong and was killed for just being a Christian.

So I am to believe that the Christians slaughtered in Pakistan under the hadood ordinance blasphemy law 395c is OK and we should submit to them. Now are you going to be subject to an Islamic government, which means submitting to Allah? Don't be foolish and take your head out of the sand enough of this foolishness.

You are commanded in Matthew 28:19 to go and make disciples out of the nations (Ten Tribes) by teaching them the Torah. Don't be unwise and don't remain caged by men's laws that are designed to keep you in shackles!

If the early believers listened to the local laws of the land of Y'sra'el then they would not have preached the truth of Messiah in Jerusalem and Y'sra'el as it was halachikly illegal to do so. These believers were not afraid to go to jail and break the law, so because of their obedience, today we have widespread biblical faith.

Here the two central commandments that Yahushua repeated regularly; was first love God then your neighbor. If Loving God means obeying His ordinance then no matter what a human king ordains, his law must be rejected if it is contrary to Torah.

**Remember whenever biblical law is being broken it overrides any local law even if you have to go to prison for it. This does not mean that we advocate violence but we advocate standing up for Torah law, which guarantees YHWH will receive honor and return honour on to you. It depends if you want to be bound to the devil or to the God of Y'sra'el. Take your pick.**

This is not sedition in which we respect where we live and try not to break the laws but our higher calling is to obey YHWH first and foremost hence why in our lives we need only have our own marital laws from the Torah and don't bind yourself to your government and be then shackled by their systems. This is exactly how they want to trap you.

Remember the following when our people of Y'sra'el were entrapped in Egypt by Pharaoh to become servants and then the Pharaoh issued a decree to kill their sons then do you think they submitted and said let's all stop having children and stop marrying?

> **Shemoth (Exodus) 2:23** Now it happened in the process of time that the Sovereign of Mitzrayim (Egypt) died: and the children of Y'sra'el groaned because of the bondage, and they cried out, and their cry came up to Elohim because of the bondage.

Notice the children of Y'sra'el cried and did not give up being married and start living in solitude.

> **Shemoth (Exodus) 3:9** Now therefore, behold, the cry of the children of Y'sra'el has come to Me: and I have also seen the oppression with which the Mitzrim (Egyptians) oppress them.

YHWH did not say oh look how lovely, the children of Y'sra'el are into the same monogamy as the rest of the nations and having a single baby policy as in China. YHWH saw the bondage and the shackles to prevent Y'sra'el from having children which would also mean a restriction in marriages in Egypt. Are you not in that restriction in Egypt (America and the nations)? Yes we are but we must act our rightful laws to get the wives and produce the children to be right-ruling and obey Torah.

The lies of Christendom of remaining single or getting a single wife like the Romans and Greeks has also gone to heaven and YHWH is not pleased. The Romans only took a wife for showmanship and to have a child but the model the Romans and Greeks had was one wife and one boyfriend in other words they were into homosexuality. Japheth has always been big in that department. You will find two things most common with Yapet, homosexuality and child pedophilia. Look how many cases of pedophilia are occurring in US and England. Celebrities are being caught out for these crimes that they committed decades ago and even today is no surprise they are still doing it.

Here is the model of Torah incumbent upon every Y'sraeli everywhere irrespective of status.

> **Shemoth (Exodus) 1:12** But **the more they afflicted them, the more they multiplied** and grew. And they were in dread of the children of Y'sra'el.

What is Em-Chukmah teaching us? The more our people were persecuted the more our people married wives and had children and they grew in persecution. Likewise brethren wherever you are make marriages to our women and have children to be right-ruling. We must grow organically to fulfill YHWH's commandments. This is a command if you did not know it. YHWH has said the following:

> **Beresheeth (Genesis) 1:28** And Elohim/Powers allotted an **Increase** upon them, and Elohim/Powers said to them, Be fruitful, and multiply, fill the earth, and subdue it: have dominion over the fish of the sea, over the birds of the air, and over every living thing that moves on the earth.

We are commanded to have children with our women and YHWH will increase you every time you take a wife, he did not say look at your finances first, he said look at me first. This is a set-apart command for us to take wives and produce children, leave the rest of worries to YHWH. In order to fulfill this ordinance you must have at least a minimum of two wives. Any less and you are against YHWH's commandments pure and simple.

I know a man who has six wives, each time this man took a wife YHWH increased him financially as money came in either through a salary increase or some other benefit given to him so do not be deceived by the goyim (heathen nations) to follow after their patterns. I have a student in America who I challenged to take my advise and go get an additional wife and to prove me wrong. He went to get another wife and after he got the wife he told me that he was given a pension for life of $2700 each month. Alongside that he also got a lump sum of money.

He said I put you to the test if what you taught about YHWH is true or not and I found that every word you have written is true. I had another man question me on the principle and he followed the same to get an additional wife. I told him the greatest mitzvah you can do is to go get a widow and marry her as you will get great benefits. The man who is my student did just that and received tremendous spiritual and financial increases in his life and confirmed them to me. So I tell you the Y'sra'eli reader, do not fear, YHWH will help you, put his principle in practice and you cannot go wrong. When the children of Y'sra'el were distressed, persecuted they took their wives, they had an average of seven to eight wives and fifty two children each. They did not stop and think well maybe I can have my one wife and one child. Such policies are of Satan and do not work but only add to diminish our people.

We must do what YHWH has commanded. Look at the opposite end the Muslims are increasing organically and the enemy has prospered while our people slumber and rot in prisons because of their foolishness. Stop this foolishness and come out of the mentality of Egypt and Greek theologies that only look at repressing us. Stop sleeping around with gentile women who give you no hope and the children they give you are a rebellious lot. You must get those wives only who are Hebrew and or gentile converts sincere to follow Torah and then you have children with them this is our duty and our call and nothing should stop you from doing this very thing.

Some of you are thinking I don't have food on the table for one wife how can I support two. Step out in faith and see the wonders of YHWH. YHWH has said He will allot an increase so He will according to Genesis 1:18.

Let us look at Melek Dawud

> **Ruth 4:13** So Boaz took Ruth, and she was his wife: and when he went in to her, YHWH gave her conception, and she bare a son.

Boaz married Ruth and died after one night according

to Hebrew traditions, she conceived as per the plan of YHWH and Obed was born the grandfather of King Dawud. According to the Zohar Boaz came into the world for this one night to give seed for the coming Messiah. Ruth was Boaz's second wife note he too was a ruler priest. Boaz a black man took a black woman who was an Y'sraelite woman and not a gentile as many people make it.

She was living in the land of Moab prior to coming to Y'sra'el but her heritage is Y'sra'elite and not gentile as erroneous thought as gentile marriages were forbidden. She gave birth to Obed who in turn fathered Yishai (Jesse) who fathered Melek Dawud. These are all Y'sra'elite black men. The Messiah in the line of Dawud was also Black see my book Yahushua the Black Messiah.

> **Ruth 4:14** And the women said to Naomi, Benevolent is YHWH, which has not left you this day **without a kinsman**, that his name may be famous in Y'sra'el.

This was a polygamous arrangement in which Boaz took Ruth as wife being related to her. This kind of polygamy was commanded if a brother died and there was no other younger or older brother the widow would have to be married to that man to bear children. What many forget is that the child that was born in other words Obed would be called Ruth's deceased husband's son and not Boaz's son.

This command to marry a woman even if you are married is found in the Torah.

> **Deut 25:5** If brethren dwell together, and one of them die, and his wife had no child, from the dead brother, she shall not marry outside to a foreigner: her husband's brother shall go in to her, and take her to him to be his wife, and perform the duty of a husband's brother to her.

Then YHWH orders the brother who is alive to take his brother's wife as an additional wife. The reason was to give sons to the dead brother by marrying his sister in law who has no son. This way the children could get the dead brother's name and the dead man's progeny may continue in Y'sra'el. If there was no brother then even the father of the dead man was allowed to marry though this rarely happened as there is only one recorded case in the Torah of Judah and Tamar in Genesis 38. Another man from the family could also act the kinsman.

Coming back to King Dawud his first wife was meant to be Michal who was forcefully given to another by the deceiving King Shaul.

> **First Samuel 18:27** Therefore Dawud arose and went, he and his men, and slew of the Plushtim two hundred men; and Dawud brought their foreskins, and they gave them in full to the Sovereign, that he might be the Sovereign's son in law. And Sha'ul gave him Michal his daughter to wife.

First Shaul the Benjamite king had promised King Dawud a wife but later by becoming jealous he wanted to kill King Dawud.

> **First Samuel 19:11** Sha'ul also sent messengers to Dawud's house, to watch him, and to slay him in the morning: and Michal Dawud's wife told him, saying, If you do not rescue your life tonight, tomorrow you shall be die.

The spirit of jealousy that came about King Sha'ul was meant to show his ego issues and in the end to show the end of his kingdom where king Dawud was meant to rule instead.

King Dawud had at least eighteen wives and he also had marriages in the North and South forming the North/South divide patterns of our forefathers.

First King Sha'ul promised him his older daughter Merab which he gave to another by cheating him and then he promised him the younger daughter Michal as she loved King Dawud only this time to do the same after betrothing her.

When King Dawud became King he had her brought back to him as his wife.

The father King Sha'ul had twice done this by making promises then breaking them. These were not just silly promises but there was a ceremony and pomp attached to it. You don't just give your daughter's hand in marriage as a king and do it in a quiet back room but these were public events but King Sha'ul was playing dirty politics and not being truthful and honest.

> **First Sam 18:17** And Sha'ul said to Dawud, Behold my elder daughter Merab, her will I give you for wife: only be valiant for me, and fight YHWH's battles. For Sha'ul said, let not my hand be upon him, but let the hand of the Plushtim be upon him.

**King Sha'ul was trying to have King Dawud killed but what you sow is what you reap, in the end it was King Sha'ul that died.**

> **First Sam 18:27** Therefore Dawud arose and went, he and his men, and slew of the Plushtim two hundred men; and Dawud brought their foreskins, and they gave them in full to the Sovereign, that he might be the Sovereign's son in law. And **Sha'ul gave him Michal his daughter to wife**.

The bride price that was set by hundred foreskins of the Philistines which King Dawud gave two hundred instead.

Later King Dawud married two women from the North one Ahinoam and the other Abigail the widow of Nabal.

> **First Sam 30:5** And Dawud's two wives were taken captives, Ahinoam the Yizreelitess, and Abigay'el the wife of Nabal the Carmelite.

One of King Dawud's wives was in Ziklag in the south

and one of his wives was in the North later he moved with them to the town of Hebron

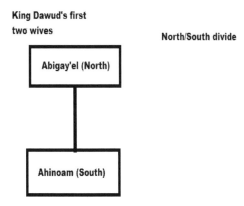

King Dawud went on to have a total of eighteen wives of which eight are recorded as follows: We are told in the book of Acts that King Dawud's tent will be raised.

> **Acts 15:16** After this I will return, and will Rebuild again the Tent of Dawud, which is fallen down; and I will Rebuild again the ruins there, and I will set it up:

This Quote is from Amos 9:11, YHWH will **Rebuild** what was fallen down, not start a new religion called Christianity that has no basis in the belief that Y'sra'el was to practice. The Hebrew word 'Binah' to build or to Rebuild has its root in the word ben for son to Rebuild the sons of Y'sra'el therefore bringing both the House of Y'sra'el (Ten Tribes) and the House of Judah (2 Tribes) in view and not some new concocted belief called Christianity that is devoid of YHWH's Torah. So what do you think God will raise up Melek Dawud and not his eighteen wives? According to Christendom it's hard for them to accept this but God will raise them all.

# Chapter 5
## *Questions and Objections*

**Objections:** Some people write to me coming out with blanket statements in opposition such as that "The Father is not teaching them this" or that "this is of the devil" or worst still "this will destroy your testimony" however not one scripture is cited against what Torah states about Biblical Patriarchal marriages. Blanket statements are quite happily accepted of Abraham being the father of our faith but it's ignored that he was a Patriarch in Patriarchal marriage system. The ironical stance of many Christians and allegedly Torah observant Messianics is comical who claim to be following the faith of Abraham but reject his lifestyle which was Patriarchal. Hello anyone listening?

**Objection:** The Father is not teaching them this. Answer: First of all the Father can only teach you what you are mature enough to handle so He will never overload you with the whole truth since you might stumble at the tiniest bit of truth. Clearly you are stumbling with your gentile cultural values versus the real Torah values. If you are still feeding on milk then how can you handle meat? Now ask yourself this if you are a Torah + Messiah believer, then how much did it take for you to give up your bacon in the western lands or even in the east if you ate it as some do? How much stumbling block was that when people with knowledge from the Scriptures came and said don't' eat the unclean foods. It could have been crabs, lobster, shrimps or some other food like maybe even horses are consumed in France. So to say the Father is not teaching you this does not make a Torah truth an untruth but shows that you may need to mature up a lot more yet. Can your ego accept this?

    The other thing could be that you are considerably in older years of your life and you never intend to get married or do not see the need to then one must ask why do you care whether it is one marriage, two or none. The only thing the Father expects from you is an Amein to His commandments just like Abraham was vindicated for being faithful with many wives and hard

Torah truths and no he did not lie when he said Sarah is his sister which is something a brother told me a while ago but I had to show him that this is simple Churchianity nonsense and that the Torah speaks of him in a very favorable position and maybe he should really consult Torah next time he speaks and then I showed him what YHWH said about him and what Abraham's lineage was and how Sarah was born and was really his half sister coming from the second wife of Terakh.

YHWH gave an incredible testimony for Abraham as follows.

> **Genesis 26:5** because Abraham obeyed My voice and guarded My ordinance, My commandments, My statutes, and My Torot.[10]

Is this the type of testimony you desire then start being Torah obedient?

**Objection:** This is of the devil and you are doing his work.
Answer: I am quite amused at this one since the ones saying this reveals to me have no understanding of Torah laws, or the Devil and how he has perverted Patriarchy to enforced serial monogamy which is pagan through and through and accepted by most Christians yet is of the Devil. So tell me where is the Devil working? How about in your Churches? Many people like this work from ignorance as were people in the first century who accused Yahushua of casting out demons by the power of Beelzebub.

This is what my Master had to say and I say ditto. Since ignorant people accused my Master then I fully expect to be accused by the same type of ignorant religious masses but the vindication will always come from the Master in whose testimony I stand.

> **Matthew 10:25** These twelve Yahushua sent forth, and commanded them, saying, do not get

---

[10] Abraham was a very good Torah keeper and YHWH gave a true report on behalf of Abraham keeping His Torah teachings.

into the way[11] of the heathens, and into any cities of the Samaritans do not enter:

**Objection:** This will destroy your testimony!
Answer: Now they have decided to sit in the Most High's seat. I have known about this truth since the day I was regenerated by Yahushua and it never destroyed my testimony then because it is not my testimony that I worry about but His for me? My testimony sadly for many ignorant people out there is NOT mine but YAHUSHUA's. It was He who worked in My life so anytime my testimony takes on any more meaning than that I am bigger or that I should be exalted may it never be because I live to exalt the Master's most set-apart name YHWH.

The whole of scripture alongside being called Tenach, Nabim, Ketubim is also called Eduth meaning <u>testimony</u> or witness. Whose testimony is the Tanak? The Master YHWH of course and the Patriarchs and prophets of our people Y'sra'el. So my testimony or witness MUST be of Him so that He is esteemed and it is for Him and never for me. Any Torah truth will always shine through no matter how difficult for us it may be.

One famous Rabbi said "Truth is buried in the grave" and rightly so because lies are rampant in the world and accepted as truth one such is serial monogamy and the other that the chosen people are Caucasians in Y'sra'el when in fact the chosen people are the black people amongst us who came out of the slavery. Like this I was also buried in the grave when I was like many Muslims dead in my sins and sure to go to the everlasting fire to the lake of fire but Yahushua changed my life with the Truth and so raised me from the grave where Truth is still buried for many.

How is that possible you may ask? Well think about it, if I never knew truth and had died then I would find out Truth after death in the grave. The criteria for accepting Truth should never be whether I like it or not

---

[11] Pagan practices from the Aramaic. You have YHWH's WAY or the Pagan 'way.' Most Christians today live in Pagan practices, which are incompatible with YHWH's WAY.

or does my spouse like it or not but simply is it from the Father and anything that is written in Scriptures I attest to being from the Father since Yahushua confirmed that it was not His words but the Father's He spoke (John 14:24).

> **Second Samuel 12:8** And I gave you your master's house, and the wives of your master into your lap, and gave you the house of Y'sra'el and of Yahudah; and if that had been too little, I would moreover have given to you more.

So who was it that gave King Dawud his many wives? The Father in heaven declares that He did or do you think King Dawud's own hand did it?

I know some truths are hard to practice simply because they bring in unique problems and logistical issues within themselves and it may be that it's not your calling so why worry. How many of you are asked to be martyred? How many of you stand at the front lines to be the first one in line to be killed hands up all who do?

I know this is not for everyone doubt many of you are willing to go on the front lines in Pakistan and Afghanistan and proclaim your faith openly. Some of you have never left the lands you were born in and don't even have a passport. I know many ex-Muslims are selected simply by the mindset we were brought up with such as dying for the Muslim deity Allah. However difficult martyrdom might be but this is one truth many people would reject if it was the tenet of the Christian faith but it is a requirement for some of us (Psalm 116:15 Precious in the sight of YHWH *is* the death of his kedoshim (saints)) to be hacked to death but not for all so since we are not afraid to die then why should we be afraid to practice other truths such as biblical polygamy. Our practicing of truth only requires me to know it is Torah law and that is enough. I do not need any denominational approval.

Admitted you may be macho behind your computer keyboards but how many of you are willing to wear my shoes and travel to the radical regions of Pakistan with prevalent suicide bombings and some of the other places like Y'sra'el and the Palestinian territories where you only see yourself as expendable for YHWH's esteem and witness.  Are you willing to make that kind of stand?  If you are not then why write vitriolic hatred against us who make a stand for ALL of YHWH's truth?  You only bring you respect down in our eyes who understand TRUTH and you destroy your testimony in YHWH with lashon hara (evil speech) against His chosen servants.

In the end patriarchal marriages actually helps 80% of the world cultures come to know truth and the Muslims are patriarchal people, it helps them to come to terms with truths such as that this is Torah based and not Qura'nic.  A Muslim Sheikh with twenty wives is likely to become a Torah based believer more so then just Christian because he is not about to divorce his nineteen wives to appease you or your denominations and at the end of the day why should he espouse to Roman Catholic dogma that the protestant churches are aligned with today.  I admit I don't aspire to taking sixteen wives but Truth must be told and practiced and I would rather stand with ALL truth then half truth as many Christians do sorry.

So for me as an ex-Muslim a faithful Y'sra'elite the God of Y'sra'el I make the best model for those Muslims who are Patriarchal and I have a lot to gain then to lose.  The sad part is that I lost not one but two families for Yahushua before and I am willing to lose another family for Him now and I also admit that I may lose some of you as friends but the reality is that I would never meet most of you so my loss though regrettable is minimum but my gain is eternal because I stand as a living testimony to YHWH's laws penned 3500 years ago for all nations especially to the 1.6 billion Muslims who still need salvation.  HalleluYah.

At the end of the day the ONLY testimony I need and want is one where the Master Yahushua says "Well done my good and faithful Servant."  You can reject me but my calling is irrevocable to the Master Yahushua using me for His call and purpose.  I was and I will always be faithful to ALL truth penned in Scriptures including Patriarchal marriage and Biblical polygyny.

## It was not so from the beginning

We often hear the term thrown around that Yahushua made in the gospels "that it was not so from the beginning", to mean we are to be one man and one woman only (Akhad in marriage) not one man with several women etc.
Let me quote the full verse.

> **Matthew 19:8** He said to them, Musa because of the hardness of your hearts allowed you to put away your wives:[12] but from the beginning it was not so.

This is breaking the back of scriptures and misquotation that usually is done by Christendom trying to derive laws out of something where no law is given.

Yahushua was not demanding monogamy nor showing it in Matthew 19:8 but showing "divorce" was forbidden and showing by analogy or kal 'v'chomer (The seven rules of Hillel) that there was no divorce allowed since marriage is a covenant/contract/agreement until husband's death while in our society we have divorce on demand by the wife who refuses to agree with anything the husband has to say on any touchy subjects not just plural marriage but to take that to mean plural marriage is not allowed is quite comical at least to me.

Now I see why the Muslims laugh at Christians and don't take them seriously at all when terms like these are thrown around without any understanding.

If plural marriage "was not so from the beginning", meant that YHWH made a law in the garden for monogamy then why isn't everyone walking around NAKED? Well didn't He show the ideal state to be NAKED? Plural marriages have always been in YHWH's mind as His perfect will since YHWH has only ONE will and not two the Christian model of man then "it was not so for everyone to practice plural marriages"

---

[12] The word is plural because we are allowed to have plural marriages as our lifestyle.

because many men are immature and cannot handle one let alone two or three wives. Each man has to make the call of what He is called to do in the Y'sra'elite community, for some it will be monogamy till their death and for others it will be Patriarchal living and no man is under the law (man made laws) to be restrained otherwise as long as they walk in obedience to YHWH.

**Question – YHWH only chose one wife so cannot have two can he?**

**Answer: Let us examine Ezekiel:**

> **Ezekiel 23:2** Son of man, there were **two women**, the daughters of one mother:

YHWH has two wives in the form of Y'sra'el. Abbah has eight wives in total, since Abbah YHWH is the first Patriarch and revealed Patriarchal marriage and the one who appointed them from everlasting because the Torah was revealed to mankind not in Sinai but always existed in heaven for as long as our Father did.

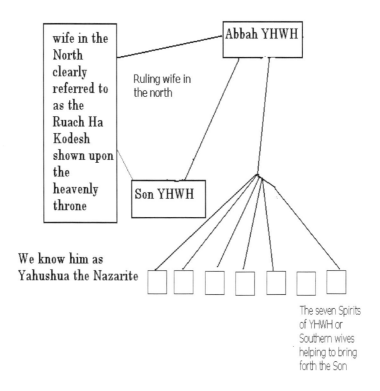

God did not say that I am taking my second wife after the first wife is divorced the act of serial monogamy but from the beginning he had eight wives but in scripture he called both Houses of Y'sra'el his brides too. His seven feminine spirits that gives an **allegorical** picture of seven concubines who were all working to reveal the only Son of our Abbah in heaven though the main principle **allegorical** wife of God meaning the Holy Spirit, the Mother or Em Chockmah who is the feminine Spirit also called the mother of Yahushua in the very earliest writings of the Nazarenes that have been hidden by the Roman Christian Church and some are believed to be lost that is if you believe in church lies.

**Objection** – The Holy Spirit is a masculine (HE) so where do you get the idea that God has male and female attributes and commands us to obey Torah which Christians believe is not longer for them but is for the Jews.

**Answer:**

> **John 16:13** And when She, the Ruach (Set-Apart-Spirit) of Truth, is come, She[13] will guide ye into all Truth for she will not speak of her own initiative; but whatever She shall hear, that shall She speak: and She will show you things to come..

**Terms used:**

**She** - The Holy Spirit is feminine and this may come as a shock to many but this is what the early Nazarene followers of Yahushua also believed. This is what Origen had to say about a text known as the book of Hebrews written in the Semitic tongue on the Holy Spirit. Origen (185-232 CE) said:

If any one should lend credence to the Gospel according to the Hebrews, where the Saviour Himself says, '**My Mother, the Holy Spirit took me** just now by one of my hairs and carried me off to the great mount Tabor,' (Origen's Commentary on John). So Yahushua called the Ruach His mother. It is important to note that in Hebrew all words carry gender whether masculine or feminine so when the translators translated these texts to Greek they changed the gender from feminine 'She' to the masculine 'HE.' When the text was translated into the English language, which has either a 'he,' 'she' or 'it' gender, this further compounds the problem because you cannot call a Hebrew word an 'it' as they have done in some places in the text. The text was naturally

---

[13] In both Semitic texts the Hebrew and Aramaic are either masculine or feminine but this was mixed up in the translation of the Hebrew word Ruach and Aramaic Rucha with an 'it' or a 'He' gender switch. The Hebrew gender of the Ruach is feminine and perfectly matches with YHWH also having a feminine side in the plurality of YHWH which is clearly evident in Isaiah 66:13 where He tells you that He will comfort you as a mother. It is clear to us looking at the Aramaic that whoever did the translation of these words deliberately chose to stick to the modified Greek mindset carrying it over into the Aramaic as well.

carried over from the Greek to the English with the incorrect gender.

**Guide ye into all Truth** - Torah truth is like a mother because she is the motherly side of YHWH. We do not know or cannot give her an earthly form, all we know is YHWH is a plurality of Father, Son and the Ruach, which shows us the picture of a family.

**Shall here** - The Holy Spirit emanated out of Abbah YHWH so will speak whatsoever the Father instructs her which is His Torah that the Son spoke about numerous times.

**Objection:** The restoration work of Messiah is to have ONE Bride (no polygamy) and to rescue her from adultery, divorce and widowhood. Y'sra'el could never be married to Messiah as an adulteress or as a divorcee or as a widow as Torah says the High Priest must be married only to a "virgin daughter of Y'sra'el."Hence the need to be "born again". Y'sra'el must become a virgin Bride. This is accomplished in two ways:

(1) Spiritually by BELIEF which causes renewal of the mind (repentance unto obedience) – which is a NEW spirit.

(2) Physically at the return of Messiah – by the resurrection of the flesh – this equals a NEW body.

**Answer:** The Messiah came to redeem the one wife that was divorced by YHWH out of the **two** wives. Scriptures does not command anywhere that the High Priest is limited to only one wife. Many people read that into the text because it is not stated. There is nothing that says he cannot be married to two wives as long as both are virgin. The requirement is that they must not have slept with any man and must be from within Y'sra'el and strictly speaking virgins. The two wives are the House of Judah and the House of Y'sra'el.

       **Leviticus 21:13** And he shall take a wife in her

virginity.

The High Priest is limited to marrying a <u>virgin</u> only but there is no number limitation. Most of Y'sra'el's High Priest's were monogamous but that was by choice and not commandment.

If we strictly apply the criteria to the son of limiting him to one wife then what are you? You the reader are an allegorical one wife and I the writer allegorically also one wife that makes two and there are millions of others. So how many wives? Now don't tell me 1 + 1 + 1 =1 like foolish Christians. That would be the wrong way of counting because many in churches count this way.

If the High Priest being also the Messiah and KING of Y'sra'el cannot have more than one wife then that by your own definition rules him out as a King and Messiah because by being the anointed one nothing anywhere says he is not allegorically married to more than one wife in fact He is. Welcome to your man made Messiah. Most of Y'sra'el's kings were polygamous, King Dawud and King Solomon come to mind but I can name you several others who had more than one wife. Y'sra'elite pattern was of patriarchal marriage and not the Satanic monogamy practiced in the West.

Is the Messiah polygamous in Allegory?

> **Matthew 25:1** Then shall the kingdom of shamayim (heaven) be likened to ten virgins, which took their lamps, and went forth to meet the bridegroom.

So what is the Messiah, the High Priest doing with Ten virgins, I thought He must be restricted to one according to some of you? From your point of view it also would mean that He rejects the laws of His Father who allowed Polygyny in the Torah after the pattern of heaven which would mean that the Caucasian 'Jesus' is a fraud according to Christianity and not to be trusted because He allegorically is polygamous but most

Christians blindingly following pagan traditions make him out to be a false Messiah by the way he is portrayed. The Real Yahushua by the way was and is black.

> **Matthew 25:10** And while they went to buy, the bridegroom came; and they that were ready went in with him to the marriage and the door was shut.

The Marriage was consummated with the five brides (plural patriarchal marriage), while the other five foolish ones were left out. If we loosely apply the symbols to the Church then half of them are unwilling to obey Torah and unsaved already.

**Question:** If YHWH'S original intention was polygamy then why did he create ONE Adam and ONE woman for him?

Who said that he created the first woman as Chava (Eve) the foolish churches with their ignorant and bad translations?

Let's start with Genesis 1:27.

> **Genesis 1:27** And Elohim/Powers created ha'Ahdahm in their own image (s),[14] in the image (s) of Elohim/Powers created; male and female created them.

A man and woman were created here and at this point they were outside the Garden of Eden. The Hebrew word 'Adamah' means earth and not red as many have ascribed to it. The Chadic word 'dham' also means 'blood' and is associated with the dham/earth and not with a particular colour as such but to associate it with the word for earth because man was created from it. Earth mixed with the water and the first common ancestor of mankind was a black man in Africa. From him come all different races of people only possible if he

---

[14] Plural, includes the Ten lights and Spirits one being the Son.

was black, the colour white does not produce all races. Sir Isaac Newton proved through the spectrum theory only the black colour produces all colours.

The first woman that was created with Ahdahm was Lilith for his wife. Note both were created from the ground, Lilith was animated by the vapour see note Gen 2:6, while Chava his second wife (Patriarchal wife) was created from Ahdahm's side. The first woman became rebellious to her husband and ran away by using the set-apart name of Elohim, which then brought the need to create the second woman for Ahdahm and the third. This was the first sign of the North/South axis of the two wives in Patriarchal marriage which all our ancestors followed, which was the pattern later adopted by Abraham's ancestors also who were Horoites. Lilith was in the south, the creation took place in West Africa while Chava was created in the North region of Y'sra'el in Jerusalem. Y'sra'el was part of the African continent and not in Middle-East which is a modern derivate word. At that time the whole land was very fertile, which today has become the Sahara and the Arabian Wilderness. Wherever there is oil and coal today it can be proved that it was once very fertile. Note coal/oil produced from trees that were buried during the flood and compressed together while diamonds also come from coals. This is evidence of a fertile landmass.

> **Genesis 2:21** And YHWH Elohim caused a deep sleep to fall upon Ahdahm, and he slept: and he took Akhat of his side bones, and closed up the flesh there;

**The Creation of Ahdahm's Second/Third wives Chava, Ishah, the Beautiful Black women**

> **Gen 2:22** And the side with the bone, which YHWH Elohim had taken from man, he made woman, and brought to the man. **23** And Ahdahm said, at this reoccurrence, These standing in front of my face are bones of my bones, and flesh of my flesh: they shall be called

Ishah (woman), because these were taken out of her Husband.

The Hebrew word צלעת here is plural for sides, and עצם bones, and not, a single bone. Those who argue, for a single rib, can not address the Hebrew language showing us, plural bones, which indicates the creation of more than one woman at the same time.

Plural ending word for one is "akhat" versus singular ending word "Akhad." See Gen 1:9 where it is singular Akhad while here it is plural Akhat with a Tav ending instead of a dalet. YHWH took Adam's SIDE, including his flesh, which can mean more than one rib. The same word is used in building the tent; Shemoth (Exodus) 26:20. One side of the tent consisted of twenty pieces of wood, therefore, we cannot say it was a single rib. This is assumed by many; but is simply presumptuous and wrong. YHWH brought more than one woman but one at a time is what the text is saying in Genesis 2:22. The Hebrew text in verse 23 is Zot Ha-Pa'am (זאת הפעם) in the ancient Hebrew hieroglyph Ha Pa'am has the character of the Heh for nostrils ⌐, the Head for Peh ●, the Ayin to walk ∆ and Mem for plural waters or the water container ⊥⊥. Both the word Zot and Ha' Paam are plural words, which is indicative of plural women standing in front of him. It means not just one woman but women standing in front of him since one is called Chava and the other Ishah. The Heh is not just for 'The' but "THESE" meaning more than one was present. So then this second wife of Adam was Chava and the third wife of Adam called Ishah would have also given birth to children and it is from these that the daughter of that woman who would be the half sister of Qayin would have been legally married according to the Torah while incest is forbidden Lev 18:9. The word Pa'am can also be translated faces of people which also points to a plurality of women.

God did not just create one woman and actually more than one because many people out there have made God sinful and your present laws will have God in the jail. You have accepted the ridiculous that God allows incest when he forbids it from the beginning. How can Qayin marry his own biological sister (Gen 4:17) and God be okay about it? That is what most of you have accepted and you then go on to define God with your standards.

The Hebrew word Ishot can also denote a wife or wives plural, normally the word Ishah meaning woman is used. In the Hebrew language there is no word for wife so this is the mystery so Adam could have been calling her his wife and not just a woman, these were two women created here one which was placed in the North axis and the other which was placed in the south axis, see Genesis 12 and Genesis 25 of the Hidden-Truths Hebraic Scrolls for an explanation of the North and South meanings. The word Aysh from Ishah means 'fire' or something 'hot' so the idea of a woman also envelopes her passion towards her husband. The shin character is also used in the name of the sun for shamesh hence the women are also the esteem of the man. A man has to keep each wives heat/passion in control through a loving relationship. Polygyny was present in the Garden and those who hate it don't see here two women were created to avoid incest from the beginning. YHWH indeed does not change Malachi 3:6, only the wise understand this. A biological brother and a sister who are from the same mother and father cannot marry, which is a sin but a brother and a sister from different wives of the same husband are allowed to marry as was Abraham and his wife from Terach's second wife see Gen 11:29 and Gen 20:12. Ruler priests always had two wives minimum.

All God did was to create one man and one woman with subsequent women to show how a sexual union takes place in the Garden. So when two are made <u>one</u> flesh it means sexual union between one man and one woman at one time. That also rules out a man having sexual intercourse with two wives at the same time because it is at <u>one</u> time only to avoid any unwanted results or consequences of jealousy in women. So a man can be Akhad with more than one wife just like God is Akhad with us individually those that have a relational contract with him and there are seven billion of us on this planet but he is Akhad with us individually at least those that are his So a man can be Akhad with wife number one and his subsequent wives as well without any issues. God is Akhad with the Ruach Ha Kadosh who we call Im Chockmah or mother wisdom and God is akhad with the seven Rachamim (Spirits). God is Akhad with his Bride the House of Y'sra'el (wife number 2) and God is also Akhad with Judah (Wife number 1) allegorically too.

Was God Akhad with the two allegorical brides or not? If He wasn't then let's talk and if he was then this argument cannot stand about Adam and Chava being one. These presumptuous arguments only come from untailored western minds stuck in their depravity and trying to raise up their own standards before God's set-apart standards.

This also has nothing to do with perfect condition versus imperfect being outside the Garden. Adam was first married to another woman who left him but was not divorced and then Chava with other women was created. If we believe in this then what does that make Adam marrying Chava and what are the other women? What about the one that ran away while simultaneously being married to Adam?

Was the Messiah Akhad with the allegorical ten brides of which five were faithful and five were not in Matthew 25?

Unfortunately such questions only show me people try to put God in a tin box and then pretending that God is unlimited. You limit God and then pretend you serve him and you ascribe sin to him by saying he allowed biological sisters to be married to their brothers which is always going to be sin.

These ideas of prohibiting what God has allowed long before the Garden the model He reveals in heaven also as I illustrated above that the Father as the Elder, the principle picture of the wife is the Holy Spirit and the seven Spirits the concubine picture in heaven. These problems are usually with Christian women and Christian men who claim to be Torah following but know nothing about Torah or the God they serve.

Unfortunately the women of the west have brought chaos in the Western lands by their feminist pagan ideas. Recently in the BBC News three women were challenging Ireland's laws on abortion as being wrong. So they wanted to murder their children and they went to England to murder them calling it a personal choice. Abortion is murder whichever way we twist the logic the same way the monogamous model of the west is illogical and satanic while the real model that God gave us is shunned.

> http://news.bbc.co.uk/1/hi/talking_point/8404230.stm

Ireland abortion:

Three women are challenging Ireland's abortion laws. They say that their human rights have been abused because of the country's position on abortion.

The women argue that their health and well-being were harmed because they had to travel to Britain to terminate pregnancies.

The Irish government has engaged two leading lawyers to argue its case that the country has a sovereign right to protect the life of the unborn.

So when you follow the world's way of serial monogamy then don't cry when people like Tiger wood's sleeps around with eight women apart from his wife. This is the world's way of hide and seek, while God's way is black and white. If someone wanted two wives then they go and get them and support them. No scandal and no embarrassment in the heavenly court for the Torah obedient men or women.

Did we hear any scandals of the South African president who has several wives? He is a committed husband and not just some flimsy polygamist who has been married to one of his wives for over fifty years while most of the monogamists out there hardly last a few years.

His youngest wife Nompumelelo Ntuli would put objecting Western Christian women who oppose God's laws to shame, while everyone was seeking her attention in her beautiful attire in April 2009 and she was so happy with her husband that the only words that she uttered out of her mouth were "Jesus is Lord."

In the West the errant wives run around maligning their husband's. Even the monogamous wolf varieties are busybodies to usurp the authority over their homes and want to rule the husband. They put down their husband's and steal the God given authority from the head of the household and they call that freedom over there.

These women who reject the law of our Father in heaven will not be reaping His increases but curses instead and neither will we find them in the coming kingdom.

For such women I have news for you. Wait till YHWH sets the judgment against you on Yom Ha Din (The Day of Judgment) then you will know that He indeed has spoken but you did not have the ears to hear and the Holy Spirit had left you long ago but you were not wise but you were too busy in your lives to notice this. While you were busy building your false little empires in this world, He had ousted most women like you from the Kingdom and you have no kingdom and no hope. Has anyone the guts to tell you this except me, I doubt it because only His called out ones have the will and courage to speak hard truths which makes us unpopular. I would rather be unpopular with the world but still remain in my Father's will.

Jacob Zuma was right when he attended a G20 meeting and there was only one seat for one of his wives and talking to a reporter said that the leaders of the world pretend monogamy but have secret mistresses while he was proud to be a polygamist and loved all his wives and children openly. Well that is the relationship that God put his increases upon as well and not the hide and seek one where most of the Hollywood stars of this world who have no eternal future pretend to be monogamous models of the west but are nothing but hypocrites with dozen of mistresses that will appear sooner or later which allow the tabloids to cash in on these stories.

The reality is that polygamy is normal in many cultures including the African culture and it does not matter if it was a Chinese or Japanese that brought up, Tiger Wood's because clearly his nature has not changed like any other man on the planet. How many other people especially good Pastor's have been demonized by the established dogmatic wayward Christian Church who happened to have a second woman in their lives who was single and they were demonized with adultery when it is not adultery at all and he was right but his wife listening to your foolish teachings using Paulos the deceitful apostle they rejected and broke their marriage what pity can one have for such creatures.

While the real definition of adultery is to have relations with another man's wife and not another single woman who chooses to attach herself to the Pastor or any other man is not and never can be adultery and it is not whoring either since she by attaching herself is really no more than a concubine which is an allowed relationship. She will only ever class as either biblical concubine or a lesser wife or if she marries the man then a second wife and no sin committed whatsoever.

Abraham did it, King Dawud did it whose psalms many of you sing daily and even King Solomon did it all black men and living the real African/Y'sra'elite lifestyle and no it was not the Kings alone in Y'sra'el even many ordinary Y'sra'elites had concubines and many others continue to do so irrelevant of what many think or care. The Law of God will never change for any man and it is not debatable. Polygamy will always win over monogamy with many benefits no matter what corner of the world you live in.

Countless people in Churches will continue to be hounded and put down thanks to the Roman/Greek model of serial monogamy at work which is the satanic model that many of you have accepted and put yourself in bondage to the one wife who rules you. No woman is allowed to have the man for her one hundred percent this is forbidden since Adam was created first then by definition the women that came from Adam have to serve their husbands and not asked to be served that is the right-ruling model. Men in turn are to love their wives for both service and loyalty. The proverbs 3 polygamous woman is the example of love and service to her husband with the other concubines' (maidservants) and her husband's love for her in return.

Shocking though it may be to some of you but this is how liberal Torah is but you want the world's system to scandalize people and put them down so most of you continue in your own foolishness because the real black

Y'sra'elite Torah culture believers want no part of this worldly thinking or scandals and practically we only care of what God thinks and not what society dictates. As long as we uphold the Ten Commandments and the rest of YHWH's laws we are in good standing with God rest assured.

Those of you whether you call yourself Christian or whatever who scandalize other believers who may have taken part in plural marriages of any form will be judged and thrown out of the kingdom on the Day of Judgment! Don't say I did not warn you so unless you go and apologize to those you have slandered and maligned, You will NOT inherit the kingdom, never. You want proof text then here it is:

> **Hidden-Truths Hebraic Scrolls**
> **Psalm 15:1** YHWH, who shall abide in your tabernacle? Who shall dwell in your Set-Apart Mountain?

Who will dwell or reside in God's holy Temple in Jerusalem this is about the $3^{rd}$ Temple and the future millennial reign.

> **2** He that walks uprightly, and works right-ruling, and speaks the truth in his heart.

The only way to walk uprightly is to obey and GUARD the Torah commandments and to avoid sin. Have you obeyed the Torah and told the truth or do you call the Torah only for the Jews and not for me as most Christians do?

> **3** He that does not **slander with his tongue**, nor does evil to his neighbour, nor takes up a reproach against his neighbour.

**He that does not slander with his or her tongue-** Stop check. So if you have gone around the houses slandering those who were trying to live with their two or more wives in a Torah way, You are going to be thrown out of the kingdom! Go and read Psalm 15 again. If you slandered a good husband in plural marriage with the approval of other men and women and you all went around making scandals you are already evicted <u>from</u> the kingdom, your ministry is worthless you are only deceiving yourself and your time is running out, unless you repent, you will stay out. You may have slandered a brother or sister for other reasons such as jealousy the result is the same even for a run away jealous wife who hated her husband for asking to have a plural lifestyle if he could afford it and she subsequently forced a divorce upon him will also be judged by God. Note all men can afford plural marriage. There is a secret principle I will explain later.

It maybe that the person you slandered did not have two wives but you slandered him or her anyway, be prepared to be ousted, the Messiah's blood will not save you on the Day of wrath or on the Day of Judgment. You will <u>never</u> be allowed to stand in the assembly of the right-rulers such as Abraham, Ishmael, Isaac, Jacob, Moses, King Dawud and King Solomon, all these men were black and their culture was black. First you rejected our men then our culture and then you run your Caucasoid culture of Japheth who is a deceiver speaking with two tongues and if this is what you have been doing then you will have no chance. Notice I did not ask your approval before writing this book because only YHWH's approval is needed.

For those of you who may not know that it was King Dawud who wrote this Psalms by the inspiration of the Holy Spirit (Im Chockmah) and He is still going to be the polygamous king upon His throne in Y'sra'el when he returns because with Him God will raise his plural wives also. He will sit as co-regent King in the millennium (Jer 30:9).

Now your only recourse before you die is to go to that person you slandered for plural marriage and apologize and ask forgiveness, make restitution with him/her first then from Yahushua after the person forgives you then you will surely be allowed to dwell in His house or its bye, bye. It does not matter if you are President of the US or Chancellor of the exchequer, you slander a Torah believer on polygamy or any other issue then you are already seen as expelled from the kingdom. Do not say on the Day of Judgment that no one warned you in the past. If you have read this far then you have been warned and the very bible that you have in your home will be used against you on that Day as proof against you. It does not matter if that Bible is the KJV, NIV, RSV or the Gideon's because it cannot hide our forefathers' lifestyles, which has Patriarchal marriages on every page. If you just like going around and being a talebearer and slanderer then the result is the same.

**Objection**: As I understand it polygamy came directly out of the wicked lineage of Cain. The polygamy of the Fathers of the faith was tolerated by God as were many other things not His original intention?

**Answer**: Read my post above you are on the wrong foot. God does not have two laws one for polygamists and one for non-polygamists. We never had monogamy so monogamy is from Satan while polygamy is from God. If you carefully look Satan is married to one wife the whore of Babylon (Rev 17:1) but he cannot replicate the Torah right-ruling model.

God has two brides not that He had them and they still exist. God with the Holy Spirit and the seven other Spirits of God are one big family of a picture of a husband, a wife and seven concubines in the very heavens where the light of God dwells and a Son dwells namely the Messiah. It is a happy patriarchal family order, it always was and will be whether you are in His kingdom or not.

There is nothing in scripture that writes the way most of you out there think. I would like to see where it has been stated by God that he tolerated polygamy only after sin? What nonsense is this? Only foolish and ignorant people devoid of Torah education have these ideas.

Now let me show you that He **delighted** in our forefathers, of who many were polygamous.

> **Deut 10:15** (KJV) Only the LORD **had a delight** in thy fathers to love them, and he chose their seed after them, *even* you above all people, as *it is* this day.

Clearly contrary to many God delighted in our fathers even though they were polygamous households being fully endorsed by God. The model of polygamy is one of heaven in a picture format. This is not to say that God is a man and has several wives but He demonstrates it like that in our human way of understanding in His set-apart Scriptures.

Who were our fathers?

- **Abraham** – Called God's friend and was polygamous with four wives.
- **Isaac** – Abraham's son who accepted polygamy for his son Jacob to be married to four wives or did you think Jacob never asked his dad's permission to marry his second wife Rachel instead of Leah? Isaac had two wives in the north and south divide too.
- **Jacob** – He was polygamous married to four wives and called Right-ruling.
- **Miriam the mother of Yahushua was the second wife of Yosef who had one wife in the south alive so Miriam was in right-ruling relationship with Yosef endorsed by YHWH.**

**Objection:** I would like to point out that king Dawud was actually very undeniably in contravention of the Torah command for Kings who were specifically told "Do NOT multiply wives to themselves." (Deut 17:17) The reason why I understand YHWH did not hold Dawud accountable for this particular transgression is because Dawud had done it in ignorance as the Torah had not been regularly taught or available to him. Only later on in Dawud's life did he really become properly mindful of the Torah. He loved YHWH but he did sin in ignorance by doing what the world around him was doing, before He fully repented and began to love and seek Torah (Ps 119)?

**Answer:** Once again this questioner is very wrong. King Dawud knew more Torah then all the kings of Y'sra'el put together. He studied it for 28 years of his life. His father was a prominent judge on the Beit Din (House of Judgment) of Y'sra'el. He was one of the four leading judges of the land of Y'sra'el. First get your facts right then make assumptions.

> **2 Samuel 12:8** (KJV) And I gave thee thy master's house, and **thy master's wives** into thy bosom, and gave thee the house of Y'sra'el and of Judah; and if *that had* things.

So who was giving King Dawud many wives, the Father in heaven or King Dawud's own heart? Now coming back to the passage of Deut 17 from where you construct such wrong doctrines.

> Hidden-Truths Hebraic Scrolls
> **Deut 17:17** Neither shall he greatly increase **many wives** for himself, that his heart turn not away: neither shall he increase a great amount of silver and gold for himself.

Many wives: This is the same principle as in verse 16. The king can have many wives because Y'sra'el was a polygamous society and that is the only way they could multiply and increase the seed in the earth. The idea here is that you must not increase wives to forget YHWH. You could have 5 fives or 15 wives and that would not be a problem as long as you could provide for their needs and be able to serve YHWH. This does not break the concept of Yesod Ha Briah of procreating seed.

The case of King Solomon having one thousand wives shows us the problem was not the 1000 wives contrary to most scholar's opinions or biases but the fact that they some of these turned his heart away from YHWH because many were heathen. So even If you being a believer marry a non-believer, and she turns your heart away from Elohim as can happen then that one wife is too much.

We have a perfect example in scripture of this one wife, who caused folly in Y'sra'el with King Ahab and his wife Jezebel. She did more damage in Y'sra'el bringing in Baalism then any other woman. Proving that one wrong wife was too much. Whereas if King Ahab had married twenty right-ruling Torah women there would have been no problem.

In Y'sra'el the argument was not whether polygamy was allowed or not but it is a reality we live and our forefathers lived. Even in the coming Messianic kingdom there will be polygamy. See Isaiah 4:1, which tells us that the ratio will be seven women to one man.

**Objection**: Moses was not polygamous. As for Moses – well, as far as I know the Scriptures never state that he had two wives at one time. We are only told that he married twice. Zipporah may have died before he married the Ethiopian. At any rate there is no sufficient Biblical verse to categorically state Moses was a polygamist. It simply can't be proved either way.

**Answer**: Perhaps you can say that for yourself that it cannot be proved but It's rather sad that time and time again I have to show misguided people that Moses indeed had not just two but three wives. In fact he lived his live happily with Zipporah and his Cushite wife before he died and no these were not the same women because he actually married the Cushite before he left Egypt and she rejoined him after the Exodus. The Cushite woman was a princess his half sister and Zipporah was his cousin wife. The North/South pattern also was followed by Moses.

One more thing the Cushite woman was a descendant of Ham while Zipporah was a Midian and descendant of Shem, these are two completely different genealogies. So the scholarly types out there who think they know better you don't.

**Yashar 72:37** And all the people and nobles swore unto him to give him for a wife Adoniah the queen, the Cushite, wife of Kikianus, and they made Moses king over them on that day.

**Yashar 72:31-32** And they placed the royal crown upon his head, and they gave him for a wife Adoniah the Cushite queen, wife of Kikianus. 32 And Moses feared YHWH Elohim of his fathers, so that he came not to her, nor did he turn his eyes to her.

**Yashar 76:4-6** And Adoniah the queen said before the king and the princes, What is this thing which you, the children of Cush, have done for this long time? (5) Surely you know that for forty years that this man has reigned over Cush he has not approached me, nor has he served the Gods of the children of Cush. (6) Now therefore hear, O ye children of Cush, and let this man no more reign over you as he is not of our flesh.

Moses never consummated the marriage with this Cushite widow queen but he had been already married earlier to another Cushite princess. Zipporah was his third wife in the scheme of things.

Moses knew Torah well enough not to consummate this marriage because it was most likely given by Cushite customs and not Torah customs. We can see that this was confirmed later when Adoniah rebelled against Moses for him not following her and her false idols of worship that she had been following.

Tziporrah was wife number three but in reality number two when we discount the Adoniah marriage but albeit became his primary wife until after which time his first wife the Cushite princess from Egypt joined him.

Now Josephus also records the marriage of Moses to an Ethiopian woman. Moses was still in Egypt so this was the first marriage of Moses adding to the equation meaning he could have had three wives in total at different times.

He did not reconcile the marriage with Adoniah, he married this princess Tharbis before he left Egypt so she is wife number one and then later married Tziporrah meaning it could be that when he fled from Egypt his wife would have gone back to Cush and later caught up with him.

We do not hear anything about Tharbis upon Moses departure from Egypt so it would be second guessing what happened but my view is she was the one mentioned in Numbers 12.

> Josephus writes:
> Tharbis was the daughter of the king of the Ethiopians: she
> happened to see Moses as he led the army near the walls, and
> fought with great courage; and admiring the subtlety of his
> undertakings, and believing him to be the author of the Egyptians'
> success, . . . she fell deeply in love with him; and upon the
> prevalence of that passion, sent to him the most faithful of all her
> servants to discourse with him about their marriage. He thereupon
> accepted the offer, on condition she would procure the delivering
> up of the city; and gave her the assurance of an oath to take her to his wife; and that when he had once taken possession of the city, he would not break his oath to her. No sooner was the agreement made, but it took effect immediately; and when Moses had cut off the Ethiopians, he gave thanks to God, and consummated his marriage, and led the Egyptians back to their own land. (2:252-253)

I suggest Moses had already married Tharbis and since Tziporrah's death is not recorded it does not matter. Moses followed the custom of his forefathers of a wife in the North and one in the south.

**Exo 18:2** (NKJV) Then Jethro, Moses' father in law, took Zipporah, Moses' wife, after he had sent her back,

Both women lived happily ever after accepting each other and had some interesting stories to tell of Moses prior to the run off from Egypt and the run in with Tzipporah's family, which is another lengthy episode best held dear in my memory.

Moses was a black man and so were the majority of Y'sra'elites we have ample evidence to know that Moses knew Torah well before it was officially codified at Mount Sinai since he refused to consummate the marriage with the widow queen Adoniah. Moses was not exactly the Caucasian Charlton Heston but a man of Negro descent. The Negro race came out of Shem while many of you are still chasing after Japheth the deciver and calling him Jewish and chosen when he is neither.

**Question:** Abraham simply did what the people around him did until YHWH actually called him. The Torah does not tell men to marry more than one woman. It only tells them the righteous way to treat those poor women if they have already married them!

**Answer:** I did not realize until now that biblical literacy is a big issue in Christendom. Christians unfortunately due to lack of good teachers have little to no understanding of many key biblical principles.

The above questioner though sincere knows nothing at all about Torah and its laws.

If Torah did not say it then how do we have our marriage customs?

We did not have to go to Christianity but Christianity had to come to my forefathers to learn and then corrupted the faith of black Y'sra'elite culture and produced a new religion from the heretic and false apostle Paul's letters.

> **Exodus 21:10** (KJV) "If he takes <u>another</u> wife, he shall not diminish her food, her clothing, and her marriage rights.

As can be seen as long as you provide for your wife number one and the other wives that you take on no sin has been committed. However the author advises caution to keep both wives in separate homes and on separate allowances so each can run her own household without coming into conflict with the other. The husband has to manage these affairs and the children concerned and the inheritance first goes to the first wife and with the first son as Torah states.

The levirate law is mentioned in Deuteronomy 25:5.

> "If brothers dwell together, and one of them dies and has no son, the widow of the dead man shall not be married to a stranger outside the family; her husband's brother shall go in to her, take her as his wife, and perform the duty of a husband's brother to her.

This was commanded polygamy both in the Tanach (Old Testament) and Renewed Covenant (NT) Matt 22:24-30.

**Question:** **Is** it lust to have more than one wife?

**Answer**: Who said lust is sin? Ah your friend Paul right? Then please I lust after food that must mean I am a sinner right? Wrong! We can and do lust after food and it is not a sin. We can and do lust for our wife or wives and it is not sin.

The only lust that scripture prohibits is lusting after another man's wife not lusting after your own (Matt 5:28)!!! The actual translation of the Greek word for lust in Matthew 5:28 is Strong's G1937 ep-ee-thoo-meh'-o, which means to long for, to covet, to desire, and to feign. The context of the word is to "desire". So if I desire food one may put it as 'lust' but that is the present English meaning however there is no sin in desiring food as is not desiring a second wife.

When the gentile translators mistranslate the bible then this becomes lust but is the word "desire."

> **Mathew 13:17** (KJV) For verily I say to you, That many prophets and righteous men have **desired** [ep-ee-thoo-meh'-o ] to see those things which you see, and have not seen them; and to hear those things which you hear, and have not heard them.
>
> If we mistranslate this as have other gentile translators then this would become 'many prophets and right-ruling men have "lusted" to see those things…

So to use the language of the KJV these prophets lusted after the kingdom so were they sinners? No. Lusting for the right thing is not a sin. Let me show you an example.

> **Luke 15:16** (KJV) And he would fain [ep-ee-thoo-meh'-o] have filled his belly with the husks that the swine did eat: and no man gave unto him.

God showed the prodigal son was starving and he was desiring or even lusting after food. Was he wrong to do that? No, in starvation he had all the right to desire after food or even lust after it as such. All the word "lust" really in context means is to desire something. So next time you desire to be with your wife or desire to be in a particular restaurant lusting after these things you will know that I educated you that it is not wrong and definitely are not sinful.

Don't you desire for your Sunday roast before it has been made? Well maybe not, maybe you eat Monday roast. (Smile). Good for you.

**Objection**: How can there be plural marriages in the Millennial Kingdom when Yahushua clearly stated that "In the resurrection they neither marry nor are given in marriage but are as the angels in heaven." (Matt 22:30).

**Answer**: Let us take a look at Matthew 22:30 once again.

> **Matthew 22:30** For in the resurrection they neither marry, nor are given in marriage, but are as the angels in shamayim (heaven).[15]

Yahushua was clear that while people are being raised marriage will not be an issue as the resurrection will be like the twinkling of an eye. It will be very fast happening in a split second at that time. But people in the kingdom will marry and be given in marriages. The questioner did not ask will they have wives in the kingdom but they asked what would happen <u>IN</u> the resurrection. Yahushua put them on the right path, that you will be like angels because we will fly like them at the time of our resurrection, but once we are raised and established in Y'sra'el we will have wives and children. It's like asking what will happen when you stand behind a red light. Well when the light goes green you go but then what happens after you go? That is similarly to the Kingdom there are marriages, houses, and children.

So if there are no marriages then how come we are eating and drinking and having children? Let me show you

> **Isa 65:20** (KJV) There shall be no more thence an infant of days, nor an old man that hath not filled his days: for <u>the child shall die an hundred years old</u>; but the sinner *being* an hundred years old shall be accursed.

How can a child die if he is not born and we are all like angels? Children will be born.

> **Isa 65:23** (KJV) They shall not labour in vain, nor bring forth for trouble; for they *are* the seed

---

[15] Many manuscripts miss or omit 'of Elohim.'

of the blessed of the LORD, and their offspring with them.

Children will be born of right-ruling believers.

> **Isa 4:1** (KJV) And in that day seven women shall take hold of one man, saying, We will eat our own bread, and wear our own apparel: only let us be called by thy name, to take away our reproach.

Many right-ruling believers will have seven wives because of the great war will leave much devastation and the need to take in more than one wife will be much more prevalent according to the law of the Torah so no new law needs to be established hence why there will be children and rejoicing in the coming one thousand years reign.

Yes Isaiah chapter 3 speaks of the Great War that Y'sra'el will be fighting in the end of day that is real Y'sra'el and not the fake Y'sra'el with its fake Jewry today. The majority of the Zionist white Jews in Y'sra'el are not real genetic Y'sra'el as real Y'sra'el were people of colour and not lily white. So those of you running to that culture and rejecting our real Y'sra'elite black culture have a lot to answer for in the coming world that is IF you even get a resurrection. Many will not.

Now you have to ask yourself if you are a prejudiced man or woman who hates olygamy then what should you do? I would suggest you repent for your sins which will weigh you down.

The only way then for this to resolve is to petition the Most High for wisdom and direction. Just because a person has been abused by say male or female spouses this has no bearing on God's law. One bad man or two bad men cannot change God's holiness into lasciviousness.

These commands were written to protect women in the African culture where the price of a woman is less than water. Where she is treated like dirt and can be kicked out anytime from her house. Where she could

even be thrown out for bad cooking. YHWH is set-apart and just and wants to protect the ones he created lovingly.
In the African culture women have suffered many abuses and God wanted to protect the women but men being what they are have still managed to abuse them. This is man's fault not God's.

What if I don't like this law of God?

We are not asked to like or dislike the law of God but we are asked to say amein to it. If we don't accept it then we are in danger of rebellion and rebellion is the sin of witchcraft. Many women have already gone that way so please I adjure you to petition and seek help from Yahushua the Master. If you do not like it then I am not asking you that you have to accept polygamy in your life but I am asking you not to rebel against God and His holy laws because rebellion will lead God to remove you from His will and it is a bad thing to be out of the will of God.

One woman said to me that she would rather not be in the kingdom where God allows seven wives to one man. It's clear to me that such a person is hurt from the past but is judging God for something they have yet no understanding of. It's a sad thing to say such a thing because that person does not have any idea of the tortures of hell/she'ol and how you never want to be in the portions of hell. Please see my article on hell in www.african-israel.com at Ask the Rabbi about Hell.

**Note:** Why did God call the Messiah a lion and not a wolf? A lion is a polygamous creature while a wolf is highly monogamous one. In fact the wolf is always identified with craftiness and Satan in scripture is the wolf. Do you see where the model of the monogamy only crowd ends up with? In the world of Satan for sure. In God's sphere polygamy is marriage whether we are happy about it or sad. King Solomon married many wives and to some of you especially ladies he was lusting, well even if he was, lust towards the one you espouse to marry or are married to is very scriptural and right as its should be called 'DESIRE". As I showed you earlier even through the Greek's usage that to "desire" your wife or one you are going to marry is very normal.

**Question**: Are you saying these things because you are practicing polygamy and you want everyone else to be like you?

**Answer**: I did not have to put this question here but I wanted to make something absolutely clear. I accept all of God's laws no matter how hard they look to most of you and polygamy is a valid form of marriage. Whether I practice or not is a personal matter and of no consequence to anyone out there. For many in the west it's not the issue of polygamy but getting the right wife and many are stuck in their ill paths of monogamy so unless women repent and turn around they are the ones to continue to suffer in society. Just as monogamy is legal polygamy should be legal while they have made the two satanic models legal that is monogamy and same gender marriage.

**Question)** If I want to marry a woman who is married in a gentile church or government system do I need to go see a rabbi for a biblical divorce before I can marry her?

**Answer)** No. She is not even married in the eyes of Abbah YHWH. You just need to ask her to go get a civil divorce so she may be free in the eyes of the government else she would be nothing more than a concubine and she is not a wife in the Torah sense until you give her a Ketubah. However nothing stops you from courting this woman if she is divorced or about to get a divorce as this is only to satisfy her local govt requirement and not the heavens.

Question) I got married in a public registry does my marriage qualify?

**Answer)** No, not in the heavens it does not. You are just a concubine type of woman down here and until you turn your marriage contract into a Ketubah your contract of marriage is not valid in the heavens. If you are a concubine here of a believer and he swore an oath to take you and keep you then you are a valid concubine by Torah law and can have relations with your said husband but have no inheritance rights until you get a Ketubah.

# Chapter 6
## *World's government systems versus YHWH's Torah government*

Many of us who are in exile have got so used to this way of life that we started to call good what was evil. The systems that the governments in various countries have devised are not for man's good but to control man so that he or she does not get out of hand. Many people in and out of Churches who are pretty clueless about God's word really have no interest in the real government that YHWH established. They pay lip service to God and run after their local and national systems as if they were God given and they are not.

It is these same people who run after their national governments who have let them down time after time yet we are told not to align ourselves with any gentile systems of government or worship hence why at the End of Days Y'sra'elites will become a menace to the government for exposing their false systems and they would not know what to do with our people. It is already been prophesied in Mikahyah what is coming.

> **Mic 5:8** And the remnant of Yaqub shall **be among the nations** in the midst of many **people as a lion among the beasts of the forest**, as a young lion among the flocks of sheep: who, if he goes through, both treads down, and tears in pieces, and none can rescue.

The remnant, the true Black Y'sra'elites will be in many nations in other words gentile nations like Europe and America where you do find them now as well here they were taken as slaves in the North Atlantic Slave trade organized and conducted by the Sephardic/Ashkenazi Jews who call themselves chosen and are not see my book World War III – The Second Exodus, Y'sra'el's Return Journey Home for more.

They will be like lions and the gentile people will be afraid of them as the Spirit of YHWH will come upon our people giving them courage and strength to overcome any gentiles.

> **Exodus 23:32** You shall make no Contract/Agreement with them, nor with their powers.

We are forbidden to lining up with government systems that enslave us further. We are not to make any covenant/contracts with them which mean if their system or their laws enslave us we are to refuse it and unwind it. We are to refuse to vote for parties that have unruly laws or laws that break the Torah laws. We are not to bind our self yet I know many of our people are bound by them and have made agreements with the heathen which are forbidden and subsequently these people have suffered. Let me give you a scenario.

You marry a gentile or believer according to the local government laws. She then subsequently divorces you and then sues you in court for all the money you got. So now what did you get? Or you may say I will do a prenuptial agreement and limit my damage but not all prenuptials are enforceable as some have limited value. Now let us do the concubine scenario or ketubah scenario only. You get a ketubah or enact a verbal contract for your wife/concubine. Tomorrow she wants to divorce you or leave you then she cannot use the local law courts to sue you as you are not bound to any of their laws. So which one protects you more? YHWH's way and not the heathen's way. Next time think carefully and in agreement with your wife unwind the local heathen contracts all of them and put into place YHWH"s laws that both benefit you and give you all a greater protection.

A woman may say what is the benefit in it for me. Well you are not to be married for a financial gain as many gentile women are doing to make marriage and then break it to bankrupt the man and take away all that he has. If that is your intention then you deserve nothing but if your intention is honorable then even with a ketubah you can agree with your husband to be what compensation will there be in the event of a divorce or separation and you can have this written in the ketubah for your security.

If the man is a man of integrity then you can also make a verbal agreement too what will he do but its always best to write it down so that if later one party forgets what was said and done it is written down and no one has forgotten about it as people can forget what they said ten years ago or twenty years ago but once you enter a marriage with a ketubah you should always enter with the intention to remain married for the reminder of your life unless one party has fallen foul or become unrighteous. Even if you sign a piece of paper and keep for this purpose to know in the likely event of a separation or divorce what obligation the husband has upon the woman and his children so you are always protected and have peace in your life.

The marriage contract of the heathen is also the same when we marry according to the heathen custom and bind our self as I explained earlier we are then giving away our rights to them. They can bind us with their laws and then dictate that we cannot have any further marriages unless we get out of the first marriage so the first thing we need to do is remove that heathen marital contract in agreement and understanding with our wife which means taking a State divorce and enact a Torah contract by getting a ketubah through a believing Rabbi.

The ketubah is the only contract YHWH recognizes and ensures YHWH is the third partner part of the marriage to uphold it. If your marriage was done by the State through another minister your marriage is not recognized above in the heavens. Your woman although your wife by the laws of the land is no more than a common law wife to you as YHWH is not part of it. This then is no more than a verbal agreement between two people with no input from YHWH which also means you cannot receive the full benefits from YHWH.

All heathen contracts bind you against Torah. If the heathen contract does not bind you against the Torah then one can say fine I will take it upon myself but usually they all do.

If you are married to a woman with a contract according to the Torah then your marriage is recognized and you are allowed to take on more wives the same way by a ketubah. If you are taking a piligesh (concubine) then you need only make a verbal agreement and it is fine and acceptable before YHWH. Usually piligesh verbal contracts also lasted a long time the women never really left their husbands in ancient times unless some grave disagreement occurred. When it is YHWH's contract then you are not bound to the heathen laws. The heathen laws bind you and your children to all sorts of government schemes and limit you to what you can do. YHWH's laws do not do that so always look to enact YHWH's laws in your life these will make you the best off.

If you already have a ketubah and a government contract then unless it is necessary to do so unwind it. Sometimes some couples may need to keep it for a short while for instance if you had to bring your wife from another country the you need to prove your marriage and they would want to see a local government marriage contract. In this case you would have to enact the contract for a short while. When your wife has been allowed to live in the land where the husband is then she gets her visa and permanent stay at which point you can unwind the government contract and free yourself. You still have the ketubah so no worries. In the governments eyes you may be divorced and or just living together and that is fine in order to protect yourselves from local harsh laws.

### How do we know if a marriage is working according to Torah and is according to YHWH our God?

According to Torah in marriage in a perfect headship the woman must be submitted to her husband and the husband must be submitted to God that would indicate a patriarchal pattern of headship and a marriage centered in God. God must be involved by words to be invited into the marriage with the following seven benedictions.

An elder or a Rabbi must recite the blessings for the couple and if a Rabbi is not available then the husband needs to take charge to recite them.

1. Benevolent are You, YHWH our EL, King of the universe, who creates the fruit of the vine.
2. Benevolent are You, YHWH our EL, King of the universe, who has created all things for His glory.
3. Benevolent are You, YHWH our EL, King of the universe, Creator of man.
4. Benevolent are You, YHWH our EL, King of the universe, who created man in His image, in the image [of His] likeness [He fashioned] his form, and prepared for him from his own self an everlasting edifice. Benevolent are You YHWH, Creator of man.
5. May the barren one [Jerusalem] rejoice and be happy at the ingathering of her children to her midst in joy. Benevolent are You YHWH, who gladdens tsiyon with her children.
6. Grant abundant joy to these loving friends, as You bestowed gladness upon Your created being in the Garden of Eden of old. Benevolent are You YHWH, who gladdens the groom and bride.
7. Benevolent are You, YHWH our EL, King of the universe, who created joy and happiness, groom and bride, gladness, jubilation, cheer and delight, love, friendship, harmony and fellowship. YHWH our EL, let

there speedily be heard in the cities of Judah and in the streets of Jerusalem the sound of joy and the sound of happiness, the sound of a groom and the sound of a bride, the sound of exultation of grooms from under their chupah, and youths from their joyous banquets. Benevolent are You YHWH, who gladdens the groom with the bride.

Note these increases should generally be committed by a Rabbi but only in certain circumstances where the presence of a Rabbi is not possible can these be taken upon yourself and done but someone may still have to stand in as an elder to do this. The greater increase is to invite a Rabbi a teacher of authority to do it. We discourage the use of local laws as they bind you.

The husband would say the following "Our Father in heaven we invite you to be the head of our marriage and both me and my wife we submit to your headship and authority. We bind our selves in the Contract/Agreement of marriage to walk in fellowship and to walk under your set-apart laws to fulfill our obligations as a married couple to you as your son and to my wife as her husband and for her to me. I as the authority over the home will deal with her faithfully in all the matters of our life in our sojourn upon this earth until Messiah comes prudently and with right-ruling ways.

Today in our world most of the marriages that we see typically are not centered in God but only in self wishes human hypocrisy or at other times just cultural bondage.

In Muslim culture many times women are married but are completely unhappy because the men want to rule women and some hyper Muslims want to suppress women of any authority or any rights inside or outside the home. This is why many of these types of women are trapped in unhappy marriages. If they try to break free and acquire a divorce then they become outcasts in that society where divorce is seen as a stigma for a woman which means the poor woman has to live the life of bondage as an unhappy person for the remainder of her life hoping for the best. No one should be in that situation.

While the opposite side of which exists in the west is where divorce is seen as trendy and the women have no control over their emotions and expressions and they feel the best way to demonstrate womanhood is to stand against the husband who dares not listen to their rules and when the men object the result is divorce. These are what I term the two extreme sides of marriage. One side where the man may suppress the woman in a Muslim or Hindu marriage and the other in which a woman suppresses the man In the name of freedom and democracy.

Both of these are fundamentally flawed and evil in nature against the Torah of YHWH.

There is a term called balanced marriages in these societies but usually the balance will tip more in the favor of women which still breaks the patriarchal headship model. If a man in the west wants his marriage to last then he has to be the servant of his spouse or else at the threat of divorce to be removed from his own home where the woman has the greater rights. The question is what God sees as a balanced relationship.

In God's balance a woman is only married to a man when they both come before Him and make him a partner in that marriage. YHWH does not recognize a marriage in a human court where he is not involved nor welcome because that is nothing more than what a society may accept and has adopted for the purposes of their local laws.

While most societies are not Torah based therefore YHWH has no basis in these relationships that is the simple fact of the matter.

If people want to argue that God is there simply by being invoked as the term God or Jesus then I disagree because in those same offices homosexuals are also married then is God in those relations also? This is where most people do not have an answer but I do he is not there and does not support secular marriages. His absence is enough to suggest that is only a human institution.

The reality is that God is not in any human institution which he has not ordained by himself so we cannot create an institution and do all sorts of unrighteous acts and then claim that the institution is approved by God. The reality is YHWH's institution is YHWH approved and recognized by Him. All Rabbis who are ordained by him or the judges of God's court are approved by him and even though they may sometimes make wrong or bad judgments but God has approved that institution with a constitution called the Torah.

The Torah mentions a man by the name of Chanoch (Enoch) and we find further evidence for Chanoch extracted from the book of Yashar that he was so loved by the people for his wisdom and wise council that he learned from God by being Torah observant. The people the local princes and kings had set this man as king over them and did you know that he had the longest recorded peaceful rule in history because every judgment that he made was Torah centered. He was a man of colour by the way just as King Solomon was later and Chanoch lived in West Africa.

He ruled over the people for two hundred and forty three years with Torah yet today our society is littered with problems including in alleged Christian countries because the Torah is not held high and is shunned and considered simply a book of legal codes. Chanoch taught all those people the Torah yet in most churches you will be lucky to get a cursory reading of it how shameful for our society and the clergy.

I consider myself very fortunate because of Torah and the contracts that are in it because if they were not there 3500 years ago then I may not be writing this today.

It is like this that my authority as a Rabbi is centered in YHWH, he called me into my present life and He ordained me in 1998 to walk with Him so by this we can tell if Torah is valid or not.

Did you know if it was not for YHWH's truth and right-ruling I have no desire to lose half my family just on a whim and go through the heartache of seeing my loved wife depart from me and lose my children? This a small price to pay to be ordained by Him in 1998 when one day he told me to follow him after a brief episode in my office in London one afternoon in a bank called Nomura International right next to St. Paul's Cathedral. It was the time of the festival of Tabernacles when my episode occurred. YHWH showed me who I belong to and that I must enter the booth His sukkah, I did not understand why he called me but now I begin to see the bigger picture more clearly.

Now do not forget marriage is a contract and when you bring your marriage before YHWH and ask him to partner with you then it is YHWH who is involved in that marriage. The husband and wife both must submit to YHWH first and then the wife submits to the husband in love. The western women do not like the word <u>submission</u> because they think of it as a bad word but in reality without submission there is no joy in marriage.

The submission is not a one way street where the man suppresses his wife but in this submission it is certainly servile where the wife loves the husband for him having the headship and also that her husband is submitted to the Father in heaven and does his best to please his wife in all areas of the home. I mention service because the wife cooks, cleans and does the household chores looks after the children, which is a fulltime and difficult job which proves her love to her husband and a commitment to the relationship but the husband at the same time truly loves his wife for her humble character and lavishes his love upon his wife or wives so the relationship is never of one opposing the other or I am better than you kind of attitude. It is inevitable and whichever way we look at it that man was created first and the woman next. Before both of these

YHWH existed hence both must submit to the higher authority and in this we are shown the patriarchal order of a household.

Typically in marriages where the women play a dominant role and the wife takes charge and breaks headship is one in which any children are likely to rebel and also not follow proper authority. The reason for this is simply this that because the wife broke the headship the rest of the order is also broken. The only way to fix this order is for the wife to repent before the Father in heaven and for the husband then to take the proper charge of the household. Even if the husband is ill or dysfunctional in some way the authority can never be transferred to a wife and remains with the husband until his death which is the term of the contract.

What if the husband or wife runs away?

In either case even if one party runs away and breaks the contract then if there are children involved and one in which hardship will result to the wife or husband in this case a husband or wife could set a time limit of the return and if no return is possible then they could seek to divorce however YHWH is clear that in a marriage the contract is till death but mercy is allowed and you are allowed to break the contract if one party has become unruly or wicked according to the Torah.

However under special provisions of the contract rabbinic authority could be used in unjust marriages to have the Covenant terminated because of breach as one where the husband refuses to support his wife and children or is unjust to his wife in some way.

This injustice must be established from the Torah and not from worldly systems.

These provisions are only brought in because of injustice and can be acted to free a woman from an unhappy and unfulfilling marriage. This means the contract is breached and can no longer be termed marriage but has become a bondage to one party since the man may not submit to YHWH or the woman many not submit to YHWH. Then either party has to seek help. In the first place its best to go back to the Creator and pray for a peaceful amicable resolution where the guilty party can accept guilt and fix themselves this is the best solution but if the guilty party refuses to own up then the rabbinic authority can issue a Get (a Hebrew divorce).

Many women in western Societies opt for a civil divorce but make note a civil divorce is not valid in the sight of Elohim if the marriage was committed under His authority however as I explained earlier that if you never involved YHWH then your marriage is not recognized by him in which case you do not need a GET since he does not see it nor recognize it but if at any time in your marriage you did make this into a Torah marriage then it is incumbent upon you to absolutely acquire a GET without which you are not terminating your marital covenant. In a civil marriage you acquiring a divorce simply satisfy your country laws to allow you to marry the next man but in Torah it has to be a ketubah or you simply tie your relationship up as a concubine without a written contract.

If a husband is obedient to the Torah then he should be well aware of the terms of the Contract/Covenant and what it means to be in breach. He must go before God and repent of any wrongdoing or injustice to his wife there is no other way around this. If the wife is at fault then she must do the same. She cannot run away and hope that she can go and live somewhere else and continue her relationship with another man this would be rebellion and adultery. In the case of the man if he is at fault and though he can go on to marry another woman but because of his injustice he has allowed his good wife to go without the marriage in which case she may seek another man for marriage and inadvertently commit adultery for which the guilt is upon the husband. If the woman was never married to the man invoking YHWH's name then her civil divorce will satisfy her civil requirement to allow her to remarry.

What if the wife simply acquires a civil divorce and walks away and marries someone else?

If this happens then she is guilty of committing adultery in which case her new re-marriage is not valid but is null and void in the sight of YHWH. If she has acquired a GET from her husband and or because of injustice a Rabbi has issued her a GET from the husband then her subsequent re-marriage is fine in the sight of God because the agreements of the marital covenant were violated and therefore a solution was sought to terminate the agreement. Please note all contracts are for life meaning to the end of one's life. No covenant can be terminated a Rabbi can bring an order of justice to a situation of injustice but really has no authority to terminate a contract of marriage. So in affect what they do is show that because of violation of the marital contract by one or more parties the contract cannot continue with safety unless one person's life is put in risk therefore the contract is not technically terminated but simply not continued under its own provisions.

When we look through the pages of scripture we do not hear of a divorce until Ishmael sent his wife back to his father's house likely to correct her disobedience and if she fixed herself she could return or the marriage could potentially terminate. We also note Moses's wife Zipporah left or a separation occurred and then later she returned when she realized her mistake, the issue was Moses's first Cushite wife and Zipporah was the second wife.

Melek Dawud's wife was taken away by force and issued a GET without his knowledge by his father in law king Shaul as the reigning monarch (Second Samuel 3:14) but he got her back even though she was forcefully married to another man. YHWH divorced the Northern House of Israel the ten tribes which was seen as a bride but even YHWH will reinstitute the marriage for which His Son Yahushua died to reconcile her back. The southern tribes such as Judah remains the wife of YHWH even though acting unfaithfully but after punishment returned back to Torah.

Therefore Torah marriage is not a joke and a game to be played and it must be seriously taken to reap the increases in the couple's life.

Once you have committed your marriage through the said increases mentioned above then you certainly have a Torah based marriage and in order to terminate such a marriage one must give a GET.

Hopefully this gives you some idea of why it is so important to be bound in God's holy law the Torah so that we may remain faithful to him upon his earth and be just and merciful to all people in our lives.

Yahushua commanded us to obey the Commandments the question is, are you willing? Torah is life and the Messiah personified it. Now if you want kingdom rewards and to be in eternity then it is incumbent upon you to be obedient to the Torah of the Master in heaven. Look at how many people in the world are Christian but simply living lawlessly putting their eternity in danger of losing everything.

> **Matt 7:21-23** Not everyone that says to me, Adoni, Adoni (Master, Master: Lord, Lord), shall enter into the kingdom of shamayim; but he that does the WILL OF MY AB which is in the shamayim. **22** Many will say to me in that day, Master, Master, have we not prophesied in your name?[16] And in your name have cast out demons? And in your name done many wonderful miracles?[17] **23** And then will I profess to them, I never knew ye:[18] depart from me, you that work Torahlessness (Negaters of the Torah of Musa).

So where is the WILL of the FATHER found? It is to be found in the Torah.

---

[16] Using the name 'Jesus' but here it is more about authority than the actual pronunciation of the name. They misused His authority and He rejects them as Torahless.

[17] To the average Christian their life revolves around miracles and they have no real understanding or knowledge to obey Torah.

[18] They knew of Him but He had no relationship with them. There will be many Christians on the day of resurrection not granted entry for remaining in continual Torah Transgression. The second qualifying text is 1 John 3:9. Read footnote Matt 5:19.

> **Deut 10:12-13** And now, Y'sra'el, what will YHWH Your POWER require of you, but to fear YHWH Your POWER, to keep the halacha in His way, and to love him, and to serve YHWH Your POWER with all your heart and with all your soul, **13** To keep the commandments of YHWH, and his statutes, which I command you this day for your good?

What is Halacha and what commandments? All the ways he set for us in the Torah and all 613 of his commandments derived out of the Torah that is the will of the Father. It's not for us to pick and choose like a buffet.

> **Deut 28:1** And it shall come to pass, if You shall listen carefully to the voice of YHWH Your POWER, to Guard and to do all his commandments which I command you this day, that YHWH Your POWER will elevate you high above all nations of the world:

The word 'shomer' for Guard means to protect and to obey the commandments. The protection is like your own property and right. Do you guard His commandments like you guard your son and daughter or your most material prized possession? The meaning behind this is like a solider standing with a machine gun guarding and fighting for his country and the rights of his nation.

# Chapter 7
## *Marriage is not an Enterprise*

In this day and age I have found many people are treating marriage as an enterprise/business in setting up prenuptials and what happens if this goes wrong or what to do if that goes wrong. This all may seem to be fine to the couple and normal but actually it degrades marriage as it is a Contract/Covenant that is meant to last the lifetime of the believers involved.

I have found many gentile converts into our faith of the western nation persuasion make plural marriage as an enterprise and by teaching that you can add on wives and then those wives can work and bring in extra income thereby increasing the household income. So for example a man gets one wife then he has one extra income then two wives then two extra incomes followed by three, four and so on by making each wife work that your income exponentially expands. This is thus cited as a benefit to this arrangement.

Let me start by saying that in this kind of arrangement what is seen is the husband then does not work and makes the wives go to work while he sits at home and takes the role of a woman, we will talk more about that in a minute.

This has a western definition too and it's called pimping. This kind of method is not the Hebrew method. Our ancient forefathers did not make all their wives work as in the traditional sense of the word. If all wives worked then who looked after the children?

There are a number of purposes of taking on plural wives one of the foremost purpose is to have many children to raise Torah based right-ruling children. In addition, the purpose of having children and the many wives that are involved then gives the added benefit that they can help out each other in bringing up these children with several helpmeets to help the mothers as friends being sister wives. The onus for the finance is still on the husband and not on the wives.

Why the western way of doing plural marriage is flawed.

God made man and made woman the Hebrew text said "male and female created them." (Gen 1:27)

Another crude way to say this is that the man had a member and the woman had a hole. In other words the actual meaning is masked not to offend others but the man was a giver and the woman was a receiver only. This is the spiritual role assigned to the man.

If the man then swaps the positions and makes his wives work and he himself sits down and takes on the role of the woman then there is a role reversal and this can cause a spiritual disaster because what is not meant to be can happen.

In this circumstance the man becomes the woman (receiver) and the woman becomes the man (giver) and this then makes the home an unhappy home due to the spiritual principle being broken. In such a house you will start to see tensions and the breakup of the family rather than the make up of the family. Even in monogamous models where the man does not work and the woman works the woman then starts to assert authority and before you know it there is a divorce. A woman may say to a man what is it that you can give me when I am the one giving it to you, I go and work so I don't need you any longer. A woman is not designed to go out and work in this hostile worldly environment, her role is to stay in the home and look after the children and look after the home.

Yes she may want to get some experience of the world in which she may for a short time work or do part time work just to get the feel of things. She may on the other hand do voluntary charity work to allow her to help some organization which may as well also be godly work such as helping the poor children in some third world country or even local to her nation. The men who think their wives have to work are wrong and they need only look at the western nations to see the high divorce rates should be a wakeup call to all of you. This is why the high divorce rate because you have made the women wear men's shoes which they are not meant to. This causes women then to assert authority over the man and before you know it the home is broken and a divorce has taken place.

No man likes to be told what to do by a woman but by making your women work you are asking for trouble and to be told what to do. The fault squarely lies with you. In the Islamic culture the Muslim women are not allowed to work and it is frowned upon by traditional Muslims. The same principle is with traditional Judaism while both modern Islam and modern Judaism allow their women to work and the same story with divorce has started to happen in these faiths.

Why you should not allow your wives to work? When you do the work you bring in the finance and means to run a home. It may be that for a short period you may allow your wife to work or you may ask her to work part time just so that she knows what it is like to work in case the man dies earlier than the woman and she may have to fend for herself. The best placement for a woman is to do entrepreneurship where she does not do the work but others do as a businesswoman.

A man must <u>never</u> take money from a woman. By taking you become the receiver then the spiritual role reversal as the disastrous affect where the woman becomes rebellious; she is influenced by outside forces causing problems. Let me be explicit to you. When a woman goes to work she meets other men and women at work. You open your wife to real damaging influences. Many unbelievers at work then start to manipulate your wife by telling her how they are behaving in their life what boyfriends the women have had and what they did with them. The men equally start eyeing your wife in order to seduce her to take her to bed for the one night stands or a secret adulterous relationship which only leads to disaster. How would you take it if you came home and your wife was home in bed with another man? This happened to a believer as he neglected his duty to the wife and supporting her financially. He came home one day and the wife was with the other man in bed. How terrible that she entered into adultery because her husband took another wife but then neglected his first wife.

YHWH tells us do not deal treacherously (Mal 2:14) with the wife of your youth meaning your first wife. Unfortunately this is not an isolated incident as the condition of some of our Hebrew men and women is like this that they have no patience and do not wait upon YHWH and end up committing a severe transgression. The second man in the adultery scenario was also a black Hebrew who likely did not care not to take the possession of another man and did not honour the Torah who was most probably a confused Christian, Torahless at best. If they had done this within the Biblical scenario with a Sanhedrin both adulterous parties would have been stoned to death.

Who put his wife in that dangerous position? You did because of your western way of thinking. If you did not do that then what danger is there if she was home all day looking after the home and children? No danger whatsoever. So when a man at work starts enticing your wife or when other loose women start enticing her with their amorous escapades then the end result is either your wife falls into the trap of the devil by committing adultery or she starts to do the behavior of the women at work who mistreat and rubbish their husband's then the woman will do the same.

Save yourself the heartache and don't fall into the trap. You may say I cannot afford two wives hence why I will stick to monogamy as it will work for me. I am afraid this is also a trap that many of you have not understood. Satan is called a wolf, the wolf is a highly monogamous creature but Yahudah is identified with the lion which is a highly selective polygamous creature in other words select your wives carefully with petition and right-ruling. Polygyny is in Y'sra'el's blood and no one can change it but it must be controlled and regulated with the Torah of YHWH to get the best result.

**The Secret**

If you apply the spiritual principle not only will you afford your two or more wives but you need to know what that principle is to make it work.

> **Beresheeth 1:28** And Elohim/Powers allotted an **Increase** on them, and Elohim/Powers said to them, <u>Be fruitful, and multiply</u>, fill the earth, and subdue it: have dominion over the fish of the sea, over the birds of the air, and over every living thing that moves on the earth.

Does it say fill the earth with one wife? No, foolish goyim (gentiles) who became the teachers of our people deceived them to go into monogamy and end up in all sorts of problems. The same with goyim (gentiles) women who would teach this and true Hebrews been deceived well by the Greco/Roman gentiles.

We are to see what is being taught in Genesis 1:28. Lilith the first wife of Adam after creation rebelled and then YHWH created not one but seven wives for Adam but as I said you had foolish and ignorant preachers who are teaching you only one woman was created and it's a monogamous model.

> **Isaiah 3:12** As for my people, **young men are their oppressors, and women rule over them**. O my people, they which lead you cause you to err, and destroy the way of your paths.

YHWH showed that in the future which is here now by the way when women rule over Hebrew men and young men oppress them. How do you think? By foolish teachings and western gentiles who know no better. The Europeans who lived in caves are not going to teach us Hebrews how to live. Those who claim to be cultured today were the least cultured. Go and investigate they lived in Mountains and caves that is their history.

Work backward and you will see what the perfect state to the imperfect is. YHWH only revealed to you three wives of Adam in the Garden but did not mention the other four but many of our people still live in blindness and cannot see.

Let me show you the perfect state.

Let's work backward for a minute shall we?

> **Isaiah 3:16** Moreover YHWH says, Because the daughters of Tsiyon are proud, and walk with stretched forth necks and flirt with their eyes, walking and skipping along, and making a jingling with their feet:

Here the hint is not only to the present rebellious daughters of tsiyon but also to Lilith the <u>first</u> rebellious woman who walked all over Adam destroying his household and is to this day trying to destroy his children with the foolish monogamous model.

> **Isaiah 3:17** Therefore YHWH will smite with a scab the crown of the head of the daughters of Tsiyon, and YHWH will expose their nakedness.

This is talking about both past and future. YHWH exposed Lilith for the evil she was, YHWH turned her white from her original black colour. Then she went to marry a rebellious fallen angel by the name of Shemyaza (Gen 6:2, Enoch 7:3). He was also turned white with the other fallen angels. Those of you attracted to the white colour and running away from the good black colour YHWH made you need to think what white represents for our people. It represents judgment and punishment because it was the Caucasian races such as the gentile Jews prominent in the west who enslaved back Hebrews. What ethic colour were they? They were white pale skins. The color white represented evil as you can find even today in African the African tribes wearing white masks to represent evil. Foolish children when will you learn?

Recognize the perfect order of the Garden of Eden!

> **Isaiah 4:1** And in that day seven women shall take hold of one man, saying, We will eat our own lechem (bread), and wear our own apparel: only let us be called by your name, to take away our reproach.

This is the perfect order that YHWH has revealed from the Garden he tells you Adam was with seven wives so I am going to take you back to the perfect order where women one day will be clamoring for right-ruling men. We are not far from that period.

> **Beresheeth 1:28** And Elohim/Powers allotted an **Increase** on them, and Elohim/Powers said to them, Be fruitful, and multiply, fill the earth, and subdue it: have dominion over the fish of the sea, over the birds of the air, and over every living thing that moves on the earth.

Let me break it down if you are still scratching your head with astonishment. The POWERS that is the plurality of the Ten lights in the heavens that we call Elohim will grant them an allotted increase. Who is "them". Those that walk in the Torah get the increase and those that do not will never get this special increase.

The increase comes if we decide to produce the fruit (children) to raise them to the right-ruling lifestyle of Torah. If we decide to cut or kill the fruit (no children) then you lose your increase and you will suffer with the rest of the world. This is the greatest secret in this one passage.

YHWH is clear He will increase you if you walk in right ruling provided you can maintain your wives even if you placed one wife in the North and one in the south as our ancestors understood the power behind this concept money will flow from the Master to manage the households. Yes it's the power of YHWH's Torah to those of us who understand it. How many of you have tried? I would be surprised if you have even known of such a concept from the Torah and ever tried it.

So what is Genesis 1:28 all about?

Marriage is not just a contract but an order and has the definition of a contract with the emphasis being upon God. God is actually giving you a secret and a direct promise to walk in his voice (Torah). He says listen to me and receive your increases. He also is giving you the negative which you did not read but it's there that if you do not listen to me and then you will encounter problems.

God is asking you to enter a contract with Him with a view to an increase being put upon <u>you</u> and your household if you are willing. Here is the first mention of Patriarchal plural marriage in fact clearly if you can grasp the details. However some of you will say I cannot but keep one marriage how in the world am I going to manage two wives. The secret is in the ingredients.

Let me once again show you if you want to see the secret of the North and the south it's in the passage if one can see it.

> **Beresheeth 1:28a** And Elohim/Powers allotted an <u>**Increase**</u> on them…

Where from? The **increase** comes from the North the dwelling place of YHWH. This is the area of the second wife and not the first such as Abraham's wife Sarah.

> **Beresheeth 1:28b** and Elohim/Powers said to them, <u>Be fruitful, and multiply</u>, fill the earth, and subdue it:

**Be fruitful and multiply** is the area of the south where the children and inheritance is. Now do you see it both North/South juxtaposed between each other.

The North is hidden (zaphon) while for south the Hebrew word Negeb is used which shows a pouring out over your household the actually ancient meaning of the Hebrew text.

Zaphon צפן

**Ancient Tzadi** 🦌 A living form in this case representative of man.

**Ancient Peh** ![symbol] The Mouth or voice of YHWH which is the Torah.

**Ancient Nun** ![symbol] A jar or cup to pour over.

The word Zaphon functionally meaning the "North" or "concealed" is used for the kedoshim (saints) of Y'sra'el who are hidden away in the Master's hand. Satan tried to steal the North which is also representative of your mind and conscience. He confused you and took away from you the key to happiness. Satan is cleaver but not in a good way but in an evil way. How do we know Satan did this. He had his pillars erected in the North. Let me take you to a story where Satan was shamed by Master Yahushua.

Showdown between YHWH and Satan!!!

> **Exodus 14:2** Speak to the children of Y'sra'el that they turn and camp before Pi Hahiroth, between Migdol and the sea, opposite Baal Zephon, you shall camp before it by the sea.

**Pi Hahiroth** - Mouth into The concealed heights
**Migdol** – High Tower
**Baal zaphon** - Baal in the North

Satan knows what happened, YHWH knows what happened but do you?

All three references of the Hebrew words show you this was one of Satan's principle places of paying homage to him thus YHWH destroyed the Egyptian Army here in the sea and right by the place of worship of Satan to humiliate him. Why once again the reference of the Sea in Exodus 14:2? As I told you earlier the sod meaning is the waters represent the gentile nations that were fighting with Master YHWH being subdued in this case the satanic forces defeated by the Armies of YHWH.

Negeb נגב

The ancient letter Nun is to pour out of a container like a jug the pouring out is from the heavens where YHWH dwells as a family. The ancient gimmel is the hand which is YHWH's hand used to pour out the increases. The Bet is the house from above where YHWH's Temple is. This gives us the Hebrew word Negeb now in the modern Hebrew pronounced as Negev.

**Beresheeth 1:28c** have dominion over **the fish of the sea**,

Where are the fish of the sea?

The sea is the area referenced WEST. To have dominion over the West also meant we would not be subdued by the gentiles as this was to be there area of reference but since our people chose to disobey our Abbah YHWH therefore the WEST (gentiles) were allowed to subdue us instead. Remember "fish" is a hint and sod meaning of men in fact gentile men.

**Beresheeth 1:28d over the birds of the air**, and over every living thing that moves on the earth.

The reference **birds of the air** is the sod (hidden) reference for us to understand what birds. This is the area of the East from where all the false religious systems came from as the Truth of Abbah YHWH also came from the EAST. The birds another remiz to satanic powers in this case had we stayed in Master YHWH we would not be overcome or attacked by evil powers but since we did the reverse we were attacked and killed all the days long.

I hope I have uncovered a secret for you that shows you the increases waiting to happen in your life and it's really up to you if you are ready or not.

If you took up the challenge that God has set then he makes his condition come true which is the **increase** that is allotted to you but if you never took the challenge how can you ask for the increase? This is one of the reasons why today many monogamous marriages are a failure. They are not His design but the gentile world's design just take a look at Greece and then Rome what a mess as our modern Western culture is formed upon them and is a shambles. Satan is into monogamy but YHWH is into polygyny. Take your pick. After forty-nine years of my life I can clearly see the principle at work. I have students who were into monogamy and after ignorantly applying the principles they have suddenly had a turn around, their income has actually increased in the household instead of decreasing. Is this a chance? No, this is truth. Those of my students I taught how to apply the principles are reaping many benefits out of it still and will continue to do so. Praise be the magnificent name of Master YHWH revealed in Melek Yahushua

    The secret is the North/South principle which I now have showed you right out of the verse in Genesis 1:28. Keep your wives in separate houses and by placing the wife in the North and south you will benefit greatly both spiritually and physically. I can tell you the principle works but are you willing to put the Torah to the test? Why I also advise not to keep your wives together is the issue of personal hygiene, spirituality and other things which I will briefly explain. Each woman has her own personal hygiene. Some are cleaner than others. Would you as a wife want to live with another sister wife who does not like to clean the kitchen, does not clean the bathroom and keeps herself in a mess? She may start ordering you around. What if you like to arrange the kitchen in one way and she does it another way? What if you are into one type of food that you like and she forces you to eat another? What if you like one particular style of paint in your living room walls and she has another? These are some of the areas where your home will break down if you are not careful.

    Well you may say I am going to make it work with all of my wives in one home, that is fine but remember the spiritual increases will never come if you function against the principles. The principles will start to work in reverse and against you. Listen to God and watch the pattern of our forefathers, none of them were poor and they all had plural wives. Show me one patriarch in the Torah who was into poverty and struggling to make a living?  You won't find any and they all had at least between two to four wives minimum.  In order for you to put the principle to effect it would be good to get two wives and then you can see it for yourself but remember be Guarding the Torah and a right-ruling husband and you will never fail.  Women who are unruly and do not submit nor guard the Torah will always fail no matter which man they tie up with and that is also a principle the gentiles do not understand. Y'sra'el is a set-apart people tell yourself that and stop behaving like gentiles.

   Did God say to you "would you like to get married to one wife?" No, many ignorant people read that into the verse and even added it.  God demanded that you enter into His increases in plural marriage by one by one in the above verse of Genesis 1:28 and the only way to do it was via a marital contract between man and woman and you can make several contracts. The pattern was well understood by true Hebrews and our patriarchs. This is why we start seeing a two wife model early on and we find this model in all people of the bible. The first wife if she had least role is not even mentioned such as in Isaac's case his first wife is not mentioned who he was married to from Yshbak's (Gen 25:2) household but Isaac's second wife is mentioned which he takes up as wife after Sarah's death.

   This means a man is not complete without marriages and neither is a woman hence why God said to Adam it is not good to be alone because if you are in that state then listen to God it is <u>not</u> good.  Go find yourself suitable helpers!!

   But its not just about patriarchal marriage but how you manage that marriage that brings in the increase. We only find out by looking at Biblical patterns how our forefathers were increased as a result of their understanding of such matters but many of us today have forfeited the increases as we have lacked to understand patterns and their meanings in scripture, even certain days are above others but Christendom has produced many errors by teaching all days are the same. Only Satan wants you to believe this and not YHWH.

In Beresheet 2:3 it says the following:

And Elohim allotted an **Increase** upon the 7$^{th}$ Day, and set it apart calling it Yom Shabbat: (Sabbath Day of rest) because that in it he had ceased from all his work which Elohim created and that needed to be made.

The word Shabbat in the ancient Hebrew is spelt with two shins so it is Shin plus Shin plus bet and Tav.
ששבת

In the most ancient Hebrew pictograph this means Shabbat or daughter of the sun. The shin is the symbol for the sun. Bet for a House and tav for the tree. The ancients preserved this by a diacritical mark of the double daggesh in the Bet. This clearly proves that the weekly Sabbath was associated with the sun and not the moon as per erroneous lunar theories. Note YHWH does not say I will allot an increase for the 8$^{th}$, 15$^{th}$, 22$^{nd}$ and 29$^{th}$ days of the month. This is the man-made lunar theory.

In headship model YHWH will allot the increase upon you and you will succeed if you are a Torah guarding man. If you have a business and your wife/wives help out this is fine but you have to be the decision maker. Your wives income should not be overriding your income in other words you should be the breadwinner and they the number two in the income bracket. If they make more money in a monogamous situation it will cause your wife to try to override you so stick to plural marriage the Y'sra'elite true lifestyle. Do not give into the hypocritical world stance on this where one man has a wife in the home and secretly has a mistress outside. The corrupt European heathen lifestyle will try to decimate you by encouraging you to enter homosexuality so you do not have any sons and daughters or worse still through contraceptives stop children. This is the receipt for disaster that is now enveloping many homes. In this lifestyle you cannot produce and it's a sin to be in such lifestyle where men who are givers become receivers. Do not enter such sins. Stick to our Torah guarding lifestyle and plural marriage. If you struggle to understand everything just get two wives and live your life with the principles I described and you will have peaceful joyous homes but learn to be loving and right-ruling with your wives, this is indeed a learning process. Also polygyny adds ten years to your life which has been proven scientifically not that I need to give science any points since YHWH said it and knew ahead of any scientist what he was telling us was good for us.

Remember with Chava at the same time other women were created after YHWH said it is not good to be alone, how come you have believed the error that YHWH only created <u>one</u> woman and that he allows incest? Do not fall into the Satanic trap. This is why the text does not say rib but Adam's side.

Remember that each baby girl and baby boy that is born all come with an allotted increase for their life. When you take upon yourself to live the Torah lifestyle the increases for each of your wife is given to you so there is no question of you not being able to afford it. The truth is you have never really tried it hence why you think this to be the case. Try it and find out differently but do it correctly North and south remember the directions and they must not be in the same house if so only for a short time. Also remember our forefathers straddled in two wives they did not always do it the same time. First one then two that is the principle secret also in that you establish two homes one after another South was first and then North. Petition the Master that he gives you the increase to do this to serve Him.

Now, I challenge you to look around at what I just said and see how much divorce there is in the western world due to the fact the women have become rebellious because they have become like men and men like women. This is a big problem. In the east where men are still men and won't allow their wives to work the divorce rates are much lower this is due to the spiritual issues I described earlier.

The spiritual issues affect all cultures and all people it does not matter what faith or religion you belong to.

Our Hebrew faith does not call us to send our women to work. If you still wanted your wife to work then don't take the money from her, let her keep her money and do with it whatever she feels like buying clothes, perfumes and Jewelry etc. But be careful if you start making your wives work and you stay at home then slowly it will lead into the trap of losing the headship and control. No home is happy where the woman works and men don't work and stay at home. If you are running a business jointly then that is a different matter and not an issue over headship.

In the model where women only work then the women start to exert more and more control before you know it they refuse to listen to you and its one fight then another and before you can even think the marriage is torn apart. If this is the spiritual issue right now in your home then take control. Go out and find a job and you do the work, tell your wife/wives to stop working and you do the work and she does the looking after of the home. YHWH does not want you to be subservient to gentiles but he wants you to be your own boss with Him as the head. In this model you will succeed a lot more, give it a try and see. No more worrying about what will happen to my job as you will become the employer and not the employed. Learn the principles and never fail.

**One home or several homes**

The other thing the western model corrupts for our men is the idea that they can round up all their wives in one home. This too will cause a spiritual disaster. Women are territorial and want their own space and time. They want affection and love. If you are all in the same home and you showed affection to one of your wives and not to the other then this can cause issues of jealousy. This too will allow the spiritual door to be opened to allow the spirit of jealousy to come into your home. Then whoever the spirit of jealousy dwells with will be the one becoming jealous but its not that you can control that in some way because once again the fault squarely lies with you. Why did you group all your wives in one home? Also the issues I explained earlier of how a woman wants to keep her home differently to each sister wife and the spiritual strength in the North and South model to receive the increases.

To encourage you further I know a man who has implemented the very model I just described above with three wives, one in Africa his south, one in the North with another in the south. This man was as all men first in monogamy and struggling to make ends meet until he came to find out he is a Hebrew man. He then wanted to apply the principles but did not fully grasp the spiritual implications but YHWH started to show him how to do the things. He started to walk in those principles, remember this man was just like you started with one wife not knowing any better and going along with the western ideology of one child or two children until Melek Yahushua jolted him and woke him up. He then went from his struggling one wife household to a prosperous three wife household. Oh, and if you thought how that is possible, his two wives are in foreign lands so he travels to be with them annually still managing them yes air tickets and flights all paid for. In fact I have known him never to be so well off, praised be the name of Master Yahushua who deals with people in right-ruling ways. So if one says this cannot work I know of this person successfully implementing it and benefitting from it.

Coming back to the argument that in one home each room is a tent is flawed at best and ignorance at worst, remember the man above never implemented this model from day one and kept his wives separate and then came his increases.

> **Genesis 12:8** And he moved from there to the mountain east of Beyth'el, and he pitched her tent, with Beyth'el on the west, and Ai on the east: there he built an altar to YHWH, and called on the name of YHWH.

Abraham pitched his wife Sarah's tent first followed by his own tent. In other words Abraham had two tents. Abraham already had two other wives one in the south and one in the North. His other wives were Keturah and Mashek. Abraham kept all his wives in separate tents and in the ancient world the tents were like a makeshift home. Within the tent you had the area for the kitchen, the bedroom the living space all partitioned separately.

Abraham had his own tent so that in times of his wife being impure he could sleep separately remember Abraham understood niddah the issue of women's menstruation. Note, Abraham was the provider for all his wives, sure they had servants but they were also provided for by Abraham so the wife in the south Keturah had no issues with Abraham visiting her when he was able to do so. He did not have to be there all the time. This is why a man can have two wives in separate countries and visit them as he has time during the year and as long as he is providing financially for their means even this model can be worked today and will succeed. This model will not succeed with white western women as they are bent on personal domination and rather be the head then allow their men to be the head.

> **Genesis 18:1** Then YHWH appeared to him by the terebinth etzim (trees) of Mamre, as he was sitting by the tent door in the heat of the day.

## What tent door?

Note Abraham sat in his <u>own</u> tent door and not outside Sarah's tent as she had her separate dwelling. Hagar his wife also had her own tent which was her dwelling.

Why are we shown this? To allow us to see how a right-ruling man should function with all wives in separate dwellings.

> **Genesis 24:67** Then Ytzhak brought her into **his mother Sarah's tent**, and he took Ribkah, and she became his wife; and he loved her: so Ytzhak was comforted after his mother's death.

As it can be seen here Ytzhak took his wife and brought her into his mother's tent proving that the mother lived in a separate tent. This was an honor and privilege for Ribkah that she had been given Sarah's tent who was the matriarch to confer favor unto her.

Things were passed down and in Hebrew culture Jewels, money and clothing would have been made prior to the son's marriage and kept for his bride for the son's marriage.

    One aspect we can learn from this episode is that if you put all your wives together in one home it can cause tremendous friction. Whether you agree with me or not the spiritual principle applies and will be in affect. Keep your wives separate and you will have a happy life, keep your wives together and you will have to deal with the constant headache and competition. The only time the wives should come together is during the annual celebrations or at other times when you wish but only for a short duration of time. You must not look for the easy way out if you want the bestowal of spiritual benefit and favour then pay heed or continue to suffer in the foolish monogamous model or worse putting up all the wives in one home. You cannot blame women for being jealous when it is you who is making the mistake.

Note Jacob learnt well from his father.

> **Genesis 31:33** And Laban went into **Yaqub's tent**, into **Le'yah's tent**, and into the **two maids' tents**, but he did not find them. Then he went out of Le'yah's tent and entered Rach'el's tent.

There were seven tents.

Yaqub had his own tent plus his four wives and two maids equals seven.

What about you?

    So rooms in one house do not equal separate tents or homes. In order to qualify for a separate home you need separate kitchen and bath facilities as well. Each tent in ancient times was equipped with these items of need.

    Also you cannot expect your wives to live on pittance and you would have to allocate expenditure for each household so there is no grief and squabbling. What you do for one wife you should not tell to the other wife keeping matters confidential between each other which also allows to remove competition. The same can apply for what one says to you then you can keep that matter confidential. This way you will have a happy harmonious relationship between your different households. At this point some of you may say I cannot afford one house then how can I afford two or more. In the case where you cannot afford the separate households the answer is obvious you are not applying the spiritual principles hence why you are struggling and worst you may not be a living a Torah centred life. What can you do, well you can be the western gentile man and live with the one wife satanic model or you can be the Hebrew man and start to change today and petition to YHWH that you want to return to the ancient paths and work at it where YHWH will make the opening for you to practice this Kadosh lifestyle.

If YHWH gives you the ability then you can look at implementing the ancient model else this is as much as you are able to do. It's no good getting two wives if you cannot afford them and then you create problems for them and yourself. You do not want to be in this position. Assess your finances carefully so they can stretch to cover your homes but first ask YHWH to show you how to do it. Remember south first and if you do north first fine but must have the southern leg to balance it out or a disaster will happen where the spiritual scale is unbalanced. If you place your wife in the south first then a few years later you can place the wife in the north this is perfect if you are able to do this. The money will be given to you provided you obey the Torah pay your tithes the secret to your financial success but not without the wives. Remember a cord of three cannot be easily broken. Let me demonstrate some of the hidden secrets of the bible.

> **Ecclesiastes 4:12** And if **one prevails against him**, two shall withstand him; and a **threefold cord** is not quickly broken.

One shall prevail against who and who is the two and what about the three?

The <u>one</u> that will prevail against him is Satan against the Hebrew man or woman who does not listen and does not behave according to YHWH's Torah. The two shall withstand him if a husband and wife in monogamy come together they barely manage to sustain the attack of the enemy but it's only the three remember husband, wife in the south and wife in the north who overcome the attack. This is the cord that cannot break in other words the spiritual principle in force of three, not two and for sure not one. Do not ever get into this pious mumbo jumbo of becoming a nun or a eunuch we are not commanded to be in such states. There is no such commandment. The best model is marriages. Women who are alone must get a covering and find a right-ruling husband you do not become complete until you join the marital family or else you will lack and you will continue to struggle and suffer heed the voice and seek that right-ruling man from help from above. I see many Hebrew women are still lacking that man and still living single, the wrong model. You were not created to be alone.

**How many days?**
How long do you spend with each wife depends on what arrangement you have made with your principle wife. The principle wife will always be the first wife that you married which you will place in the south. Any other arrivals later are secondary wives. If you principle wife insists that she needs five days with you and to allow you to use the other two days for your second wife then that is what you have to accept unless you can negotiate more days in which cases your choice is limited. You have to give your principle wife room to adjust and accept things. If you can agree a 4/3 day split in the week it's great. Usually the humble women will win even if it's fewer days they will end up getting more.

**My husband has gone astray**
The shock to most western brought up women or in the eastern cultures where polygyny and monogamy are prevalent is this that the husband has gone astray if he has gone and picked another single woman unmarried to have a secret affair with. Unfortunately most women do not understand men are designed to be with more

than one woman from the start. It is my firm opinion that Adam had seven wives created for him. The first one was Lilith who ran away and subsequently it was six more women after that event. Why seven? The Hebrew lettering indicates it and also in Isaiah 4:1 it indicates at the End of the Age seven women will marry a single man as they will have to remove the reproach from them which is producing the perfect model.

> **Isaiah 4:1**And in that day seven women shall take hold of one man, saying, we will eat our own lechem (bread), and wear our own apparel: only let us be called by your name, to take away our reproach.

So what if your husband started to like another woman that being single and not married. What is your course of action? First of all if you took the typical western approach of threatening him or ask him to refrain the more you say the more he will do it. He will not stop just because you threatened him. It is in man's design and also an Y'sra'elite even more so. You cannot take the Y'sra'elite out of a man and even gentiles have it in their design too. In the ancient world gentiles also practiced polygyny albeit without our Torah laws so it was in their own way.

**What women should not do?**
It is a grave mistake for you to slander your men or to run off to the divorce courts this is a big mistake. Even if you divorce your husband the next one that comes along he will be the same so learn to apply the situation to your advantage so that your husband will be lifelong faithful to you even if he has other wives or concubines. Its very easy to get around the law to take a wife and not to enact a local national contract and just live with a woman on verbal agreement because that is what a concubine contract is and all men can simply choose to do that and they do not break any law. In fact many are doing this right now.

The thing that a prudent and wise woman needs to do is to become the proverbs 31 woman who was polyganous and an understanding woman. She needs to sit her husband down and ask him if he is able to manage two women financially and keep them in their respective homes. If the answer is no then he will just create problems for all parties concerned so he can wait for his opening but it may be that the man is going to walk by faith and all the Master Yahushua to benefit all of you so let him walk by faith. If the man is Torah observant he must walk by faith and that even if he cannot manage them no problem call upon our Master Yahushua to assist you to do the right thing. The wife needs to be patient and let the man have time to decide the right course as he has to make the final decision since he is the head and the women need to let him be the man and the head.

If the man is able to or wants to prove that he can then the only thing the primary first wife needs to do is encourage and love her man and to tell him she is there for him no mater what. If you support your man you will keep your man for life and if you reject your man you will lose him and possibly the next one that comes along will be even worse so beware.

Set some ground rules with him, how much time will he give to you and to the other wife? Make sure that the other woman is checked out for sexual diseases so that he does not pickup a sexual disease and bring it home to you. How much you decide with him could be in such a way. If the woman is in the same city or another city it could be 4 days for you and 3 days for the second wife. If he is going to have a second wife/concubine in another country then its likely he will spend more time with you and less with her as he can only go to her a few times a year such as 2 to 4 times and possibly spend a number of weeks with her or a few months at most. Either way the majority of women run after the divorce courts you being a Hebrew woman do not make the mistake if your husband is Torah obedient but if you want to have a happy marriage with a contented husband then you need to be wise. One of the questions often comes from women is why do men go after the second woman and why not stick with the one wife for life long.

I am afraid wishful thinking gets nobody anywhere and society cannot cage men who are designed to have more wives. Either it will be with your consent or without so decide quickly what it is going to be. If you know where your man is then you will be more at ease and you need to come out of worldly thinking that you cannot share your husband because like it or not an Y'sra'elite man is going to be shared one way or another. The men do not go for the second women solely for sex but it's also change. Men can easily get bored and want a variety. So if a man has two wives he has variety and he feel contended and as I said it's in the design, remember all Hebrew men will end up in the North and south directions with wives or girlfriends I have seen it so I know. I have not found a single man yet who did not want to have a second wife and many men claim to be able to live with one wife but believe me this is a lie that men like to tell women and it's a nice white lie and they have had secret second relations privately. I would rather be upfront then to be secretive and if a wife is unrighteous she can leave that is not a loss as the Master Yahushua can add two where one leaves and he will give you submitted wives.

    Just as Sarah selected the wife for Abraham that being Hagar you need to take active part in it and not shun your man but love him and that is your role. I guarantee you this that if you love your man and stand by him he will <u>never</u> leave you and if he is a man of integrity he will always come back home to you and be with you that is certain. Do you want a different dad for your children or the same one? Rather then you rush off to the divorce court, cause yourself a pain and allow others to make money out of your troubles don't do it please. Yes lawyers are not there to support you they are there to make money from your troubles then why go through with it? Women wake up.

> **Prov 31:10** Who can find a virtuous woman? For her price is far above rubies.

    Make your price far above rubies so that your husband knows your worth and your worth is only going to be built up when you stand beside your man and be supportive to him. He is going to find another woman sooner or later for sex or for change and sex is a gift from God there is nothing wrong with it. Don't make sex into something it is not. The Church has made sex into a taboo subject but sex is normal and if a man has a healthy appetite for sex then all the better.  It's when he does not have a healthy desire then problems come in with depression, anxiety and stress.  Avoid it.  If I am wrong look at the book shops littered with marriage counseling books and most of those books are totally useless as they don't tech you what men are like and what they want. I am giving it to you here, learn it and use it to your advantage.  A man is like a lion you can tame him but even then he is going to have other lionesses apart from you. Now start looking at it from both men's perspective and God's for a change.  You have tried the world's perspective and failed but when you apply the natural design you will know things are no longer the same.  A husband respects that wife that supports him and loves him even when he has another wife and this is pretty normal and not an abnormal obsession.  It's in the design. Look even at the western world how many men are married and have mistresses. Would you rather know that your man is with the other wife and will be back at so and so time and when he returns you are there for him to love him and to take care of him then if that is you the man would be lifelong faithful to you?

    You have tried the world's way now try this and see for yourself. I would even encourage you to ask your husband that if he wants to take another wife that you have no problem with it and you will be supportive of him then see the reaction of the man and see how this man will have see you as a precious ruby in his eyes. The only thing that you need to be aware of is to set a boundary and then work within the boundary and you cannot go wrong.  Ask the man that whichever wife he brings in that you will both agree to it and that the next wife will respect you and it is the man's job to make sure that happens. Leave the onus to him then sit back and see how things pan. Assuming the man made a bad choice without your input or even with your input then the only woman the man is going to return it is YOU.

> **Prov 31:12** She will do him good and not evil all the days of her life.

You want to do good to your man all the days of your life and his life. Then you want to support him, you want to stand by him no matter what. Start telling yourself this from today and acting on it. If you follow through with it the greatest increases of your life await you. If on the other hand you reject your man, accuse him of cheating when he should be doing it with your consent then the heartache is only around the corner for you and a broken marriage. No one benefited from a broken marriage it leave scars and please don't allow it to happen.

> **Prov 31:23** Her husband is known in the gates, when he sits among the elders of the land.

The text says the husband was a well to do man a political or a public figure and the wife was so supportive of him even with the other handmaidens (concubines) that she supported her husband and loved him took care of his home. You should likewise change your thinking one hundred and eighty degrees and start to love your husband, start to tell other of his goodness to you and what his relationship means to you. If your husband is good or even bad praise him that he will even turn away from the bad habits he has and will turn to good. There is much power in the tongue and in your words. Use positive words to build him up.

> **James (Jacob) 3:5** Even so the tongue is a little member, and boasts of great things. Behold, see how a little fire kindles a great forest!

Take great care with your tongue I implore you that you do not utter words that can hurt your husband and yourself. Control it and use it for the glory of God and praising of good. Praise your husband then see how he responds. Men love praise from their wives and they in turn should praise their wives too. All you women who have gone around the houses slandering your husband now is the time to go back to that man and repent of your sins and ask for forgiveness from the man you slandered or else you have cast yourself outside the kingdom by disparaging the law of God which allows polygamy. You have likely gone around the houses to do that as you thought like the world thinks and belittled your husband and then filed a divorce by ridiculing him and putting him down with a divorce paper. You have no place to stand and time is now to understand and to turn away from such things in the future.

> **James (Jacob) 3:6** And the tongue is a fire, a world of wrong-ruling among the parts of our body, the one defiling the whole body, and sets on fire the cycles of genesis (course of human existence); and it is set on fire of Gehenna (Hell).

If your tongue is not in control with it one can set on fire so to speak and set your course to hell (Gehenna) so beware. Do not ever usurp the authority of God in your life these are His laws and not mine He will have the last word.

Put a flower pot and curse it daily and tell it you hate it. Then put another flower pot and tell it you love it and praise it. Tell the second one how great the flowers look and how beautiful it is. Try this in a real experiment that the flower pot you cursed daily will wither away and die because you killed them with your harsh words how much more a man who is there for you but all you could do was curse him, be bitter with him daily. Now the flower pot that you praised thrived why because even flowers which are a living organism reacted to the positive words. The same way your man will react to your positive words and be more positive and uplifting and your negative words will only bring him down. Make a promise to yourself to never use negative words towards your man again.

Even if he does wrong give him constructive criticism because the only reason he is going wrong is something within him needs fixing and is broken. You are his mirror and sounding board reflecting and echoing what is wrong with him. He needs to seek the Master Yahushua for help in the areas he is wrong to help himself.

This works by praising the good things to lift him up and then telling him what was negative so he does not feel put down and he will react more positively to it. Its time you throw away your self help books on marriage and start applying the principles I have taught in this book and you will never go wrong.

> **Prov 31:30** Favour is deceitful, and beauty is vain: but a woman that fears YHWH, she shall be <u>praised</u>.

This proverbs 31 woman not only respected and lifted up her husband's name but she feared YHWH our Power. Look at her and learn there is a powerful lesson in it for all of us. She was also praised by her husband which is a positive character that lifted her up.

In Saudi Arabia the Muslim women select the second wife for their husband and they give a party and celebrate when the husband get's married to the number two. Who do you think taught the Muslims about polygyny? Our Hebrew ancestors in Saudi Arabia were polygamous and they taught the Arabs, Muhammad the Islamic prophet frequented our synagogues often and sat with our Rabbis and wise men and they taught him our ways this is why you find a lot of this in the Qur'an is directly out of the Torah. Remember you can play an important part so start doing it to rebuild your marriage.

P – Persevere, Persist and Praise
L – Love and let go of bad feelings.
E – Encourage and enwrap him in your affections
A – Accept him
S – Sex is open at all hours
E – Everlasting relationship

Remember the acronym **PLEASE**.

P – Persevere, Persist and Praise

Always stand fast to your husband, persevere with him, praise him don't hurl insults at him.

L – Love

Love him always don't put him down negatively this a definite NO. Let go of any past bad feelings, start living with a positive attitude from today.

E – Encourage

Many times your husband may be discouraged from outside situations or home situations you are to encourage him always in his endeavors. Enwrap him in your beauty and love.

A – Accept him
Accept your husband for the man he is, don't try to change him to something he cannot be. Many women fail as they want to change the man to something he is not. God made him as he is.

S – Sex

Your husband should not have to ask for sex you should be there for him all the time. Men can be spontaneous and may want to make love at any time so you have to be ready. Don't put it off and make excuses as many women do, I have a headache or I have to go out, oh I am watching my favorite program. This is one of the key reason that break marriages when women use sex as a weapon. Remember you were made for man as a helpmeet and not to usurp authority from him and to try to rule him. Men like excitement in love making too so be prepared to spice up your sex life every now and then. It's not always the missionary position where you lie like a dead duck underneath as a chore and he on top like a stiff alligator. Begin the change and learn what it takes to make him happy in the bedroom and he should ask you what you like so both of you can work to please each other and make intimacy an enjoyable experience. Men need to be proactive and make sure their women are satisfied and not just look to self for satisfaction and ignore your wives needs. Intimacy is not a five minute task give it time and make it enjoyable for both parties.

E – Everlasting relationship

Remember your relationship with your husband is everlasting you have to make with him in all occasions both good and bad. Don't run away from the bad times. You will only get the sweetness of what sugar you put in to a relationship. The more you remember this and follow the principles the happier and satisfying your marriage experience will be. Forget the world how they do business remember how Y'sra'elites live and behave according to God's standard. You have a beautiful relationship only if you want it. If you trash your man everyday then don't expect a long lasting marriage. Come out of this worldview that you can shout at him or abuse him and he will still love you. He won't. Men do not respond to threats. Do not ever threaten your man. Learn to communicate with him and talk to him politely. Men respond to politeness a lot quicker then to rude women.

In relationships women want time and affection. Men need to learn to communicate with their wives affectively and give them affection. Speak nice words to your wife/wives. Do not treat your wife/wives like trash. Make them feel important and value their opinion even if you don't follow the advice they give you.

Men make sure they do give you their input. Ask your wife/wives for sharing their needs and concerns also for their input in your endeavors even if it seems unnecessary get it still.

Men the acronym to remember is

**ACTS**

**A** - Affirm – Tell her that she is valuable to you and you care about her worth. Tell her daily the things she does well, compliment her on her cooking, on other things she does around the house. Even if her cooking was bad by complimenting you can make it better by showing her how to do it in a different way. Don't be negative and harsh as this will put her off and take a while to heal.

**C** – Communicate - with your wife/wives and make her part of your everyday life

**T** - Touch - your wife/wives and caress her, women like to be touched. Let loose the stern attitude of no talk and no touch. Sit down with her to watch a movie or a drama and share the laughter together. Quality time together builds marriages and lack of time destroys them.

**S** – Special, make her feel special every now and then buy her and other wives things, do acts of loving-kindness to your wife/wives, charity starts in the home. May be she is nagging about that bad mobile phone, get her a new one. She is complaining about the dryer get her a new one. Surprise her because women love surprises. Take her to a restaurant on an unexpected day not necessarily on just birthdays. Get out of the routine will add love to your life.

Take your wives in turn to a weekend break where she does not have to cook and you can spend the time together away from busy life. Don't be a slave to your house or job so every now and then take a break taking your wife/wives in turn. Now you begin to understand marriage is about commitment with each woman you are committed to so yes it will take both effort and maturity to get past the obstacles and hurdles. The wife is a likened to a garden the more you prune and water the garden the nicer the flowers and fruits in the garden. If you do not water it then it become overgrown in a short period of time then you have yourself to blame for it. The wife/wives are the same way, water them regularly then they will be nice and if you do not then the result is your own creation.

## Additional questions that need answers

### What about masturbation is it a sin?

This question keeps coming up as people do not understand what happened to Er and Onan, the two sons of Yahudah.

> **Genesis 38:6-10** Then Yahudah took a wife for Er his Bekhor (firstborn), and her name was Tamar.
> **7** But Er, Yahudah's Bekhor (firstborn), was wicked in the sight of YHWH, and YHWH killed him.
> **8** And Yahudah said to Onan, Go in to your brother's wife, and marry her, and raise up an heir to your brother.
> **9** But Onan knew that the heir would not be his; and it came to pass, when he came to his brother's wife, that he emitted *his seed* on the ground, lest he should give an heir to his brother.
> **10** And the thing which he did displeased YHWH; in his sight therefore He killed him also.

Er never had intercourse with Tamar she remained a virgin with both brothers, he had been instructed by his mother not to give Tamar children and the brother who took her in Levirate marriage did not wanted to give her children either. Neither brother had an y sexual relations with her this is why when she married Yahudah in a Levirate marriage she was yet a virgin. The transgression was not masturbation but not having children or raising a son for the sake of Y'sra'el. The act of masturbation is never condemned by YHWH but poor Christianity and its adherents who lack understanding call this a transgression. Even you are fertile and do not do anything you will get nocturnal emission so therefore if you were not married and did do masturbation that would be no problem and no transgression is committed.

So what was it that displeased YHWH in verse 10? Not the masturbation but two things one he did not consummate his marriage with Tamar and two he did not wanted to give her sons this is what displeased YHWH as the marriage ketubah became a mockery which has the stipulation for the husband to fulfill the wife's conjugal rights.

## Is monogamy or plural marriage the original design?

When a woman gives birth to a baby girl she is not supposed to be in an intimate relationship with her husband for 80 days. This is just under three months. If she has longer post partum bleeding the length of time will extend when the husband cannot be intimate with her. For the birth of a boy the period is 40 days minimum.

When a woman becomes pregnant the first two months the husband should not have relations with his wife as the chances of her having a miscarriage are the greatest in the first two months.

The husband should not be having intimacy with his wife in the last two months of pregnancy during month 7, month 8 and month 9. This means during the pregnancy and after the husband is not able to have intimacy with his wife the short period is around two months and the longest period from month seven to the birth of a girl is four months and 20 days (two months before delivery of the child and eighty days after excluding four white days with no bleeding) or three months and ten days plus four if it is a boy taking into consideration no intimacy in month 7, month 8, month 9 then delivery followed by no intimacy month 1 and ten days plus four clean days. The man can only have intimacy after the post partum bleeding has ceased and the woman is pronounced clean with a four white days (in other words no bleeding must occur during the white days) after the delivery the forty days are up it would be add another four days to make it 44 days.

No man can withstand waiting for his wife and expect to withhold from sexual intimacy with his wife this long, this is why plural marriage is in the design and the original design. We cannot ignore these important facts. Monogamy was never in the design, hence why it is satanic as it forces men to commit acts outside the marriage which they will do if you try to withhold them.

Now note men who did not know of the above how much pain and suffering they giving their wives by having intimacy when they should not be and should really be with another wife or concubine. In a case study a lady indicated to me that her husband was intimate with her in month seven and that caused her immense pain physically but she could not say not to her husband. This soon followed with her waters breaking and she giving birth to a seven month old baby who was born premature. In such cases the man is putting the woman and the baby's life at risk. In essence the man should have been having intimacy with his other wives but because Christendom teaches men not to therefore men make women suffer because of ignorance and man-made religious teachings that have no foundation in the Torah.

### What about bride prices how much should I pay?

Bride prices is quite biblical and there is nothing wrong with paying a bride price but this has to be negotiated with the parents. it varies in different areas e.g. in China the bride prices start from $6000 to anywhere $16000. In Africa the various clans command a bride price and it varies from $2000 to $5000.

The only time you would pay a bride price is when your wife to be is a virgin. If you wife is not a virgin she cannot ask for a bride price but you can still give gifts to her and to her family.

### Do you have to tell your other wives or ask for permission?

You do not need to ask for any permission to your wife, as long as you are looking after her needs you can enter into plural marriage at any time with any lady who is single. In a normal Torah marriage the head wife would be the one who went out to look for her husband's additional wife so that wife would be the right one for the whole family unit. She would tell her husband if she had a wife for him who was suitable to the family unit. However there were also times when the husband chose the wife and then introduced her to the family unit through the principle head wife. If we look we can find examples of both, with Sarah she gave Hagar to Abraham as a wife (Gen 16:3), Jacob was given the handmaids of his two wives Rachel (Gen 30:3) and Leyah (Gen 30:9) and we also see King David who took the wives who he saw as suitable when he married Abigail (First Sam 25:40).

**Do you have to tell your wife if she is rebellious?**

In America the Y'sra'elite men are put into a lifetime of bondage by child support because of rebellious women. The best way around this is to keep the rebellious wife and go get your plural wife, do not tell her anything, Torah does not require you to ask or tell to anyone but your rabbi alone is enough to know the situation but keep the rebellious one at a distance, provide her food and clothing and let her decide to leave and keep her at a distance about information as she will not obey the Torah and neither let you operate in it.

This allows you to save on foolish gentile enslavement of child support but keep your children and get your additional wife in a ketubah therefore the state cannot prosecute you because you do not have two licenses, no bigamy is committed according to gentile law. First do not tell the rebellious wife but If the rebellious wife finds out you have another woman let her foot the bill for divorce and run around the block then she can decide to leave. You do not need to remove her from the house until she wants to leave therefore the adage "its cheaper to keep her may well be true" for such bad and wicked women out there.

If you want a household in shalom you should not be sharing all your information between different wives. Just share your very personal information to do with finances, purchases of land, material things and properties with the North and South wives only, to share all the top secret info and the rest wives should never know everything. Or another way only share with the head wife who is in the south as she came first. In the same way if most of you are thinking Sarah is the head wife you would be quite wrong, it was Keturah and it was Keturah who asked Abraham to acquire his

Northern wife to get a child. She would be the one who would have got Sarah and approved her while she is the least spoken about in the Torah as she was a right-ruling woman.

Make sure these two wives know everything about inheritance and what to do in the event of your death. If you have supposedly 7 wives, keep info flow between two co wives North/South only but the other five wives they do not need to know as they are your family unit and they can get the information from the head wife or the Northern wife. They should only need to know what concerns their household and their children.

The two wives North/South you are sharing information with only do it if they are the most trusted and are sincere and faithful in the knowledge and the rest do not need to know therefore your home will have shalom because they are not in any conflict with burdening of unnecessary information. When you share every bit of info with each wife you bring in jealousy and conflict. The wise do not do that. This is Torah. These two wives (North/South) become your secret sharers are the wives in the North and South only, any additional wives should not be given all details remember this will help you in the long run maintain balance in your homes and remove jealousy and conflict.

Let us say that if you were purchasing land or property and you named it in one wife's name because she was most trusted and would likely help all the other wives in bad times if you were not around then if you tell this to all your wives they may become jealous and cause problems but withholding info will keep them safe and secure as this wife you have entrusted you only did so as you found her compassionate to all the other wives and to help them in times if you were not around or died. If you have a large estate you may want to make a trust and make your wives trustees so there is no conflict of interest.

Wisdom pays. If you were making love to one wife you are not going to brag to your other wives how many times you did it therefore keep bedroom things private between each wife only. The same goes for other details. Most women are territorial creatures and can easily become jealous but it is your job to manage this in the home.

**How many wives can I have?**
The Torah does not cite a number. This is dependent on you and your character and ability. If you can only handle two wives then that should be your limit. If you are able to manage 8 wives then that is fine too. The average number of wives that Y'sra'elites had in Torah were seven to eight. One woman had an average of five children. You must not place a burden on a single wife to produce say e.g., ten children, this is morally and according to Torah wrong. A woman must not have more than five children, I would cut that down to two to three children per wife and no more. So if you have seven wives, each wife can have at least one child or at least two to three children.

    This mean with seven or eight wives your children will not exceed twenty one. I would recommend though scripture does not tell you to that you should have no more than 12 children and look after them, bring them up in Torah. As long as your wife has had a child you are allowed to do birth control. My advise is to use a sleeve or condom. Do not opt out for birth control pills they can be quiet dangerous for women. The Torah does not permit you to tie tubes or put a device in the woman which is mutilation of flesh. You are not permitted to do vasectomy this is against Torah law as it falls under mutilation of self neither the removal of the womb.

    The halacha is that each wife must have at least one child unless she has a birth defect. If you wanted to have twelve children then they can come from the different wives that you have. If you decide for more then that is fine as long as you know this will require patience and effort to bring those children up and not to mention finance. Unless there is a birthing issue or the wife is barren you must have at least one child from each of your wives. If she was past child bearing age then that is a different matter and in such a matter she can help other co-wives with their children and is not an issue to take her for a wife as she can bring maturity into the family unit. I would not advise on proliferating wives or children. My advise on the matter is do not exceed eight wives unless special circumstances exist to do so. Decide for yourself what you can manage without conflict.

For your information Melek Dawud (King David) had twenty-four to forty-eight wives. Some suggest 18, others 24 but the disputed figure is forty-eight. He was the most right-ruling man and after God's own heart. However he was wealthy enough to manage his household, we may not all be in King David's shoes hence decide wisely for yourselves. Remember each wife does bring an increase of her own but still you have to devote time, energy and talent to each wife so each person will have their own individual limits and its not the same for everyone.

What you see in the worldly movies such as Hollywood, Bollywood and others is that two women fall in love with a man and one ends up killing herself or removing herself at pain to marry a man they love. In movies they have to kill or remove one of the women to fit their gentile agendas while in the Torah both women will get the man and its a win/win situation for both. Why should one woman suffer not to have the right-ruling man? Do not allow any man to dictate to you that you cannot have two wives, Torah permits it and regulates it. Be wise and you will do well.

In the western culture and some eastern cultures today it has become polyamorous relations where a woman sleeps with many partners this is forbidden. However they are doing it one by one sequentially in other words they have relation with one boyfriend who gets dropped then its another boyfriend and it keeps going on. This is unwise and bad behavior of women and men are no different into serial polygamy with taking one wife then divorcing her for another.

The gentile agenda is to keep you suppressed without children and without wives. The Torah is life and freedom choose Torah and choose life always and the Messiah is in the Torah and He is the representative of it. The Messiah was born of the second wife of Yosef who lived in the North so Miriam was the Northern wife and while Yosef had a wife who was alive in the south who helped look after Miriam in her pregnancy. No one will stop a man from doing what he is designed to do but do it with Torah right-ruling and you will never go wrong. All Y'sra'elites stand firm and be strong, YHWH be with you all.

**Conclusion and a word of advice**
In any of this situation that you and your husband enter that is if your husband wishes to take another wife/concubine then this needs to strictly remain with you and him and the other woman. Do not at any cost make this public news or go around telling your relatives or if you have wives in different countries they do not all need to know this. The more you protect your marriages the more you will be happy the more your broadcast your marriages the more problems you will introduce. People out there who have no understanding of such matters will only give you their worldly advice that is <u>not</u> going to help you neither your husband so if you want to protect your marriage remember this golden rule. Protect the information about your home.

May the El of Y'sra'el guide you and increase those of you who obey Him.

Rebbe Simon Altaf

For groundbreaking articles... www.african-israel.com

**TRUTH UNLEASHED BUT CAN YOU HANDLE IT?**

You can phone or send an e-mail at the e-mail address below for any further questions. Call +44 (0) 1296-48 27 95 in the UK. Or write to africanysrael@Yahoo.com. For US dial Tel 1-210-827-3907.

For UK;
Snail mail address: Simon Altaf, BM African-Israel, London, WC1N 3XX, England (UK).

For USA;
African-Israel,8111 Mainland, Suite 104-152, San Antonio, Texas, 78240, USA Tel 1-210-827-3907

Simon Altaf was chosen by God in 1998 for the special End-Times prophetic calling. A lone voice in the wilderness, one taught by Elohim (Ps 119:120-121). He was told by Yahushua that he is from the tribe of Lewi, one of the original Semites who was called out of Islam to rejoin His people after his long exile from Iran, and then India to Pakistan to England will follow one day back to Ysrael through the hands of Melek Yahushua. His promises are trustworthy and they will come true indeed we simply await our Master's return.

For youtube teachings please go to www.youtube.com/simalt.

Our youtube channel: www.youtube.com/simalt
Paltalk: The Real Yahushua and Torah on Saturday 9am central time, 3pm UK time.

For books
http://www.african-israel.com/Books/books.html
www.lulu.com/simalt
www.amazon.com
www.createspace.com
Get one of the most accurate Hebrew Roots Bibles available; this will become your Bible of choice opening up many areas of the Scriptures, which will give you a whole new understanding. Are you ready for a paradigm shift? This is what you need to interpret the Bible accurately.

The Hidden Truths Hebraic Scrolls Complete Bible can be ordered at the URL below. www.african-israel.com. Note the excellent translation of bible which reflects our mission to Africa and the true genetic Hebrews mentioned in the bible who live in the western word such as in Europe, America and in the Caribbean islands including many other countries like Brazil, India, Iran and Pakistan. They were taken into Brazil by the Sephardic (Jews – Gentile converts into Judaism) a prophecy fulfilled in the Bible.

# We suggest you visit our website to see the following Titles:
# www.african-israel.com

**Beyth Yahushua – the Son of Tzadok, the Son of Dawud**

Would you like to know the identity of Yahushua's family the man you call Jesus? Did He have brothers and sisters, did He get married, and are not Rabbis meant to marry?

Is it true if Mary Magdalene was His wife and if not then what relationship did she have with him?

Are you fed-up of hearing objections from unbelievers such as "since you do not know who Matthew, Mark, Luke and John were then how can you claim to have the truth?" Now you will know the truth without asking your pastor.

Who was Nicodemus and what relationship did Yahushua, Jesus of Nazareth have with Nicodemus? Who was the wider family of Yahushua?

For far too long He has been portrayed as the wandering man with no belongings and no family and living outside his home with women offering him money and food. This picture is both misleading and deceptive.

Do you want to know the powerful family of Yahushua that was a threat to Rome?

Who were Mark, Luke, and Matthew? Was Luke a gentile or a Hebrew priest?

What about the genealogy of Luke and Matthew in which the two fathers of Yahushua mentioned are Heli or Jacob in Matthew chapter 1:16 and Luke chapter 3:23 respectively?

This book will give you new insights and the rich history of Yahushua. Next time you will be able to identify the ten tribes and the real Messiah Yahushua known as Jesus of Nazareth.

**Islam, Peace or Beast**
Have you ever wondered why radical Muslims are blowing up buildings, bombings planes and creating havoc? We illustrate in this book the reality of radical Islam and the end of days that are upon us. Why are our governments reluctant to tell us the truth we uncover many details.

**World War III – Unmasking the End-Times Beast**
Who is the Antichrist, what countries are aligned with him and many of your other questions answered. All revealed in this book. Which might be the ten nations of the Antichrist? What did the prophets say on these events?

**World War III – Salvation of the Jews**
- How will the salvation of the Jews come about, will they convert to Christianity or will Christianity be folded into Judaism?
- Will the 3rd Temple be built before the return of the Messiah? Analyzed and explained with the correct sound hermeneutics.
- Will we have a war with Iran and when? Considering the pundits have been wrong since the last 3 years and only Simon has been on track up to this time. What signs will absolutely indicate impending war with Iran calculated and revealed.
- When will the Messiah return, what signs should we be looking for, is it on a Jubilee year?
- Will the Messiah return on the feast of Trumpets fact or fiction?
- Will America win the war in Afghanistan? Yes and No answer with details.
- Who is the prince of Ezekiel and why is he making sin sacrifices. Can one call these educational? Read the correct answers...

- Should we support the Jewish Aliyah to Israel or is it forbidden to enter the land for permanent stay under a secular godless government?

Rabbi Simon is the only Rabbi to look at the thorny issues that no one has addressed to date while many people mostly run with popular churchy opinions coloured by bad theology by picking and choosing verses in isolation. Is modern Zionism biblical? Is Israel right to take over territories occupied by Palestinians today? Should people be selling up homes to go and live in Israel? All these thorny questions and even more answered in this book the sequel to the popular prophecy book World War III - Unmasking the End-Times Beast.

**Yeshua or Isa – True path for salvation**
Ever tried to witness to your Muslim friends and were mocked? Do you have Passion for the Muslims to be saved but not sure who to address them? Do you want to know how Jesus Christ is Yeshua and not Isa of the Qur'an? This book helps you to build a solid bridge with the Muslims. It clarifies your theological doubts and helps to present Yeshua to the Muslims effectively to redeem them.

**Dear Muslim – Meet YHWH the God of Abraham**
Truth explained, best seller step by step detailing and unveiling Islam! This book is designed for that friend, son or daughter who is about to convert into Islam but needs to read this first. This is the <u>one</u> stop to saving their soul. Don't procrastinate, get it today so that they may see what is the truth before they cause themselves to be confounded and duped into something totally not true.

**The Feasts of YHWH, the Elohim of Israel**
Have you ever asked why the feasts were given to Israel as a people? What is the meaning of the festivals and what about their purpose which is all explained in this detailed book that delves into the signs of the Messiah and the fulfillment of the feasts and how the return of

the Messiah is revealed in the feasts. Why are we to obey the feasts forever and if we do not then we could potentially lose our place in the kingdom entry! Well no one said that before but now you will see and experience an exhilarating experience of knowing what it is like to be there. How does it feel to be up all night to celebrate the festival of Shavuot (Pentecost), what does it mean and many other details.

## Testament of Abraham

Now it's time to hear Abraham's story from his own mouth what happened, how did he become God's friend. What other missing information that we are not told about is made available. Without Abraham there will be no Judaism, no Islam and no Christianity. He is the pivotal point upon which all three religious text claim right but who does Abraham really belong to?

## What is Truth?

Have you wondered what truth is and how we measure it? How do we arrive at the conclusion that what you have is truth? How do you know that the religion you have been following for so many years is the original faith? Can we examine Atheism and say why it is or is not true. We examine these things.

## Hidden Truths Hebraic Scrolls Study Bible 5$^{th}$ Edition (Complete)

The HT Complete Bible more myths busted. Over 1300 pages packed absolutely full of information - no Hebrew roots Bible even comes close this is guaranteed and these scrolls are the difference between night and day, see for yourself!!! The politically incorrect guide to the God of Israel and the real chosen people of YHWH. Are you willing to listen to what YHWH has said about our world and how He is going to restore all things back including His real chosen people hidden to this day? Many texts uncovered and explained in great details accurately and many corrections made to the many faulty translations out there making this a real eye-opener text.

- ➔ Was Chava (Eve) the only woman in the garden? We reveal a deep held secret.
- ➔ Where did the demons come from?
- ➔ Ezekiel refers to some of Israel's evil deeds in Egypt explicitly uncovered which are glossed over in the King James Version.
- ➔ Who are the Real Hebrews of the Bible, which people does the land of Y'sra'el really belong to? Time to do away with the deception.
- ➔ Did Abraham keep the Sabbath? We show you when and where.
- ➔ But I thought Keturah was Hagar, another error of Judaism corrected.
- ➔ But I thought Keturah was married to Abraham after Sarah's death, no not really. A very bad textual translation in Genesis 25:1.
- ➔ Who was Balaam, a profit for cash as are many pastors and Bishops today doing the same thing running and chasing after the Almighty dollar?
- ➔ Who were Abraham's ancestors, Africans or Europeans?
- ➔ Why did Isaac marry at forty years of age, what happened to his first wife? Rebecca was not his only wife, an error and ignorance of Christendom exposed?
- ➔ Where is Noah's ark likely to be? Not Ararat in Turkey or Iran another error.
- ➔ Who are the four wives of Abraham and who is the real firstborn? Not Ishmael and not even Isaac. Was Isaac his only begotten son another error?
- ➔ All the modification of modern Judaism of the scribes has been undone to give you what was the real text including the original conversation of the Serpent with Chava (Gen 3) unedited plus Abraham's conversation unedited at last in Genesis 18.

The legendary Rabbi Simon Altaf guarantees that this will teach you to take the best out there and open their eyes in prophecy, historical argument and theology. He will personally mentor you through the texts of the Torah, the prophets, the disciples and the apostles of Yahushua. Does any Bible seller offer this extent of training? We do. And Rabbi Simon is available at the end of an e-mail or just a telephone call away for questions that you have all this time and if he is not there you just leave a message on the phone and his promise is to get back to you anywhere in the world. We do not charge for our calls or any teachings over the phone. It does not matter if you are in India, Australia, Russia or the US or Timbuktu we will call you back.

**Sefer Yashar (The Book of Jasher)**
The book of Yashar has been translated from the original sources and with added commentary, corrected names of Elohim with the sacred names and with other missing text from the Hebrew. This will add to the gaps in your knowledge from the book of Genesis such as the following:
- What did the wicked do before the flood?
- Who were Abraham's African ancestors?
- Did Abraham have two wives?
- What relationship did Abraham have with Eli'ezer?
- Did Isaac wait forty years to be married?
- Why did Sarah die so suddenly?
- Did Moses marry in Egypt?
- Moses, what colour? White or Black.
- Many other questions now answered.

**Seferim Chanoch (The Books of Enoch)**
The books of Enoch details the fall, the names of the angels, what happened in the beginning and what was the result of those fallen angels. Where are they now and what will happen to them. He also reveals the birth of Noach and some very important details around this about the African ancestry of the patriarchs. He reveals the Son of Elohim and reveals Yahushua upon a throne. And many other important details to complete your knowledge.

**Yahushua – The Black Messiah**
Have you been lied to about the true identity of Yahushua? Have you been shown pictures of the idolatrous Borgia Cesare and may have believed that this Caucasian hybrid was Yahushua the Melek? What ethnicity was Yahushua and what race of people did He belong to? Is it important that we know His ethnicity? What colour was Moses, King David and King Solomon? We examine and look at the massive fraud perpetrated upon the western nations by their leaders to hide the real identity of the true Hebrew Israelite people and race which are being restored in these Last Days. Yahushua said <u>everything</u> will be restored and that includes His and His people's ethnicity and colour. Would you like to know because it affects your eternity and His true message then get this book now.

**Hebrew Wisdom – Kabbalah in the Brit ha Chadasha**
The book's purpose is to illustrate basic principles of Kabbalah and to reveal some of the Kabbalah symbolisms used in the New Testament. We look at the Sefirots what they mean and how they apply to some of the teachings in the New Covenant. We also look at the first chapter in Genesis and examine some of the symbols there. We examine the name of Elohim in Exodus 3:14 and see what it means. We examine some teachings of John to reveal how he used Kabbalah freely.

**The Apocrypha (With Pirke Avot 'Ethics of The Fathers')**
Read the fifteen books of the Apocrypha to get an understanding of the events both of the exile and of Israel's early history before Yahushua the Messiah was born. Read Ethics of the Fathers to understand rabbinic wisdom and some important elements of the story of Genesis. The tests, the trials and the miracles of the Temples. Without these books the story in the bible is

incomplete and has gaps which these books will fill up and give you a more complete understanding.

## African-Israel Siddur transliterated Hebrew with English (Daily life prayers)

Many times we wonder what prayers should we do when we go to bed, when we leave our home in the morning and how do we pray daily? What prayer should I do if I have a ritual bath? What prayer is for affixing a Mezuzah? Each year you wonder how to do the Passover Aggadah and what is the procedure. This book also covers women's niddah laws to give you understanding into women's ritual purity. Unlike other prayer books Rabbi Simon actually bothers to explain small details that are important and often ignored. This is one book you should not be without.

## World War III, The Second Exodus, Y'sra'el's return journey home

How will the genetic Hebrews be taken back to the land? Are the present day Jews in Y'sra'el of ancient stock? Is there any prophecy of foreigners invading Y'sra'el and inhabiting the land? How will Elohim have war with Amalek and wipe them out and who is Amalek today? Why is the Church so confused about bible prophecy?

How will the end come and why is the world hiding the identity of the true Y'sra'elites? Will there be a rapture or marching back on foot? What happens if we die in our exile? And many more questions answered. The time has come to expose the errors of others.

## What Else Have They Kept From Us?

This book is as the result of an e-mail conversation with a believer who asked me some questions and one of her questions upon my answer was "What else have they kept from us?" This was the question that led to this book because instead of answering people with small sections of answers I decided the time had come that a book had to be written to answer and address everything as it happened from the start to the end so that many may see that the deception is real and it's a deep cunning deception which starts from your TV screens, in your newspapers followed by wherever you go in your daily life. How would a person know that they are being deceived if they do not know what to look for? Its like a Ten Pound note well if you saw the original then you have something to compare the false note with but what if you were <u>never</u> presented with the original and always had the fake in your pocket then you will likely think the fake is real and this is how it is with Christianity today that is simply mixing paganism with truth. A false Ten pound note or a bad tender which will give you no value when you redeem it as I uncover it in the pages of this book. Who was Yahushua, the real Hebrews and Y'sra'el.

**The Scroll of Yahubel (Jubilees)**
The information that is missing in the Torah has been put in here to aid us in understanding the book of Genesis more. There are gaps in Genesis with what happened with Noakh? What was going on in Moses's time. This scroll allows us to piece together that information that is so important for our understanding. True names edition with many corrections made.

**Who am I?**
A Children's book to help the black Hebrew children with identity and direction in life. Many Hebrew children while looking for identity easily stray. While they search for love they end up in gangs to prove themselves and search for that missing something. When they do not find love in their homes due to broken homes often venturing out with devastating consequences, getting involved in criminal activities to prove themselves ruining their lives. This book's purpose is to help these children and even adults find themselves to teach them who they are and to find sound direction in life to secure you to the God of our ancestors where you belong. This will help change many lives.

**Paul of Tarsus - The Thirteenth Apostle**
We examine if Paul is an apostle and if Pauline epistles match teachings out of the Torah and with the sayings of the Messiah Yahushua. We also show you what the Catholic Church has been hiding from you. You may be surprised to learn that things are not what they seem and you may have been deceived all this time. It's time for the deception to lift and for you to return to the ancient paths.

**Hidden Truths Hebraic Scrolls Compendium Guide** - For those who have the Hidden-Truths Hebraic Scrolls this is a must buy to give you a deeper understanding under the text and its meaning where the footnotes are expounded upon further in various books of the scrolls.

**New releases for 2014/2015**
**Hidden Truths Hebraic Scrolls Compendium Guide, Secrets of the Hebrew Scrolls,** Commentaries for explaining Scriptural texts unleashed

**Hebrew Characters, The Power to have prayers answered-**

**Ancient Hebrew** – Functions, Methods and Meanings. Where did we go wrong?

Made in the USA
San Bernardino, CA
02 January 2014